A Concise History of Painting

From Prehistory to the Thirteenth Century

DAVID TALBOT RICE

238 plates 90 in colour

THAMES AND HUDSON

LONDON

PRINTED IN GREAT BRITAIN BY JARROLD AND SONS LTD NORWICH

A Concise History of Painting

From Prehistory to the Thirteenth Century

Contents

The two arts of painting

This book is about painting in Europe. It is a very long and also a very intermittent story, for it begins, if one can talk of a beginning, some thirty thousand years ago in Palaeolithic times. But thereafter, at least from the point of view of our knowledge, there is an enormous gap, until we can take up the story again in Crete, early in the third millennium BC. The discoveries being made in archaeology are beginning to fill the gap – only a few years ago interesting wall paintings of the Neolithic age were discovered in Asia Minor, while numerous paintings of the next phases are of course known from Egypt, and the story of the development of kindred arts can be followed thereafter in Mesopotamia, Persia and China. But in Europe the continuity is broken, and even in classical Greece, whose sculpture we know so well, painting is now represented for us only by small-scale drawings – for they are drawings rather than paintings – on vases. Of Roman work we know much more, thanks to a great extent to the overwhelming of Pompeii and Herculaneum with volcanic dust in AD 79, and thereafter, though a distressing amount has perished, a more or less continuous story unfolds itself, which becomes progressively more complete as we approach the present day. In this volume the period until about 1300 will be surveyed; the date affords a convenient break, for it was soon after that year that the new phase which we know as that of the Renaissance first took form.

The art of this phase was, broadly, an essentially naturalistic art, and for many generations straightforward representation was regarded as the essential of good art; art which did not conform to this canon was rejected. But changing tastes have led in recent times to the acceptance of other canons. The art of today sets little store on representation, and art as a whole cannot now be denigrated simply because it does not follow old canons of naturalism. We have indeed now come to realize that throughout long periods of man's history the same outlook has dominated, and a severe stylization of natural forms or even a complete degree of abstraction has in the past quite often been readily accepted. Much of the art produced during the thousand years between the decline of Rome and the dawn of the Renaissance was thus of a very stylized character; the art of Greece before the Age of Pericles was severely formal, and in still earlier phases Greek art was at times wholly abstract. Today we can enjoy these arts and appreciate their qualities in a way which was impossible for earlier generations, and in the pages that follow a considerable amount of space will be devoted to them.

But not all early art was of this type: often it was wholly naturalistic, and, curiously enough, this was the case with the earliest art that can be associated with man; namely that in the caves of the Palaeolithic period situated in southern France and northern Spain. The fact that we can associate with man in the early stages of his cultural development simple tools or implements in bone or stone is in no way surprising, for such things have almost always been produced by primitive peoples. Nor would it be surprising to find that such things bore some sort of simple decoration. Yet it is very surprising to find that this decoration often takes the form of highly accomplished representational designs, and even more surprising that these same men, as close to apes as to human beings in appearance, were responsible for a considerable number of paintings and engravings on the walls of their caves, even though their stone implements were crude and clumsy in the extreme. Some of their products strike us today as little less than miraculous, even when their age – some thirty thousand years – and the primitive level of those who produced them is left aside. Why was it that at this very early stage of his development man turned his hand to art at all? How was it that he was capable of producing works of such outstanding excellence?

I doubt if it will ever be possible to answer the second question any more than it is to explain the gift of genius. At best one may note that a delight in copying nature is something very deep-seated in man's make-up. From the earliest times likenesses of inanimate objects to living forms have been recognized and expressed, chance resemblances have been seized on and accentuated. The constellations afford a case in point, for the men who studied the stars in early times noticed that in their relationship one with another a resemblance to some living form was to be remarked and by joining-up the nodal points they completed this resemblance and gave names to the complexes so formed – the Bear, the Twins, and so forth. Indeed, they even produced actual drawings of these living forms on which both the stars and the lines of linkage were included; we know some of them from the Moslem world, but their prototypes doubtless went back to a very much earlier date, especially in ancient Mesopotamia, where the interest in such things was highly developed.

Again chance resemblances to some living form was often apparent in natural objects, and some of these could be easily accentuated by adding a little here, removing something else there, till the resemblance was complete. We see actual instances of this in the Palaeolithic world, where the chance resemblance of a piece of bone or a lump of rock to some living form has clearly been made more conspicuous by man. The same process, a stain in one place, a crack in another, may well have inspired the first painting, for did not Leonardo say that the most inspiring model was an old wall, marked by the pitting and discolorations of time, while the nineteenth-century water-colourist Richard Wilson preferred a well-matured Stilton cheese! It was not a very long step from this process of accentuation to the production of the first wholly original work of graphic art.

1 The most recently discovered Palaeolithic paintings are those at Lascaux. Not only do they depict animals with remarkable vividness, but some show scenes with several animals, or even animals and men together, forming a true pictorial composition

CHAPTER ONE

Prelude: art's prehistory

Had this book been written in the mid-nineteenth century it would have begun with an account, drawn largely from literary sources, of the origins of painting in ancient Greece. The author would have hazarded the guess that earlier ages had produced nothing that could deserve the name of art; and would probably have pointed out that the earliest attempts at representation – cult statuettes and pictures of divine beings – were rigidly stylized and that it was only with the Greeks that anything like naturalism was achieved. The art of primitive peoples, in so far as it was studied, would have tended to confirm such a thesis.

This neat and plausible story has been completely contradicted by the discovery of the cave paintings of southern France and northern Spain. They are fantastically old. They go back not three thousand years but thirty thousand – so far in fact that it was a long time before the learned world could bring itself to accept their authenticity. And they are wholly naturalistic, more so in some ways than the art of the Greeks, of the Renaissance or even of the nineteenth century. Their discovery was totally unexpected. It is impossible to trace any connexion between them and the art of later times, but such is their

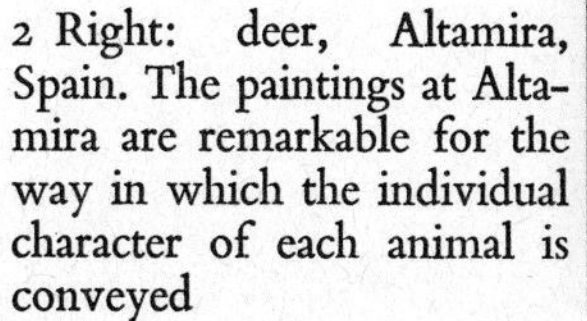

2 Right: deer, Altamira, Spain. The paintings at Altamira are remarkable for the way in which the individual character of each animal is conveyed

intrinsic merit that it is equally impossible to ignore them. Through them we get an isolated, fortuitous glimpse into the prehistoric world. What do we see?

We see animals, the animals which Palaeolithic man hunted and upon which his life depended. They are on the walls of deep rocky caves, shrouded in perpetual darkness. They are painted with mineral dyes, mostly black, brown and red, often with the contours and modelling indicated by engraved lines. The most impressive series, in spite of sensational discoveries made at Lascaux as recently as 1940 (*Ill. 1*), are still those at Altamira (*Ills. 2, 8, 9*) in northern Spain, which were first found in 1895. The paintings – those that survive are on the roof – depict animals of various species in a variety of positions and sizes; most of them are from four to seven feet long. True, there is no understanding of composition here, and the various animals that are depicted are shown higgledy-piggledy, without any relationship to one another, like a series of studies in an artist's sketch-book. But the individual figures attest quite amazing powers both of observation and of the ability to record that observation – not to mention the power to give to the renderings a remarkable degree of spirit and expression. A wild boar, ready to charge is not only clearly recognizable, but is also possessed of all the strength and vigour that such an animals must have had in the eyes of a hunter who was armed with nothing more than a rough stone club; a deer (*Ill. 2*) has all the gentleness of the breed, and one senses at once the light, bounding character of its movements; a bison is the very epitome of massive strength, a ponderous, almost immovable mass, which nothing could stop (*Ill. 9*). But most impressive of all, perhaps, is the dying bison (*Ill. 8*), its legs curled up under it, its tail still twitching; one feels that at any moment it might give one last, convulsive kick, before the heart finally stops beating and the muscles become rigid. Never has the spirit of these animals been better conveyed in art; never have details like the bison's hooves been more economically and more successfully depicted. And there is too a real feeling for three dimensions in these figures; the farther legs are clearly removed from the nearer ones, the far horns stretch deep into the background behind those on the surface, the bodies have depth and weight.

3 Bison, Niaux, France. These paintings were in all probability an aspect of hunting-magic. Palaeolithic man drew spears sticking into the sides of animals that he wished to kill, just as witches were supposed to stick pins into wax dolls to cause illness and death

Indeed, it would be hard to find animals more accurately or more expressively rendered, and the competence of these paintings, in contrast with the primitive character of the artefacts of the men who executed them, is truly amazing.

Another astonishing fact is that these paintings, and others like them, are on the walls or roofs of caverns, sometimes hundreds of yards from the entrance; how could they have been done with the aid of no more than a guttering lamp burning crude animal fat? And why were they done in such inaccessible places? Other paintings which have long since perished may of course have existed where they could have been seen by the light of day, and the presence of similar engravings on pieces of bone which were used for practical purposes shows that some of the art at least was associated with everyday objects. Such work was no doubt intended for enjoyment and delight. But why was that in the caverns done in places where it could never be properly seen? Was it the work of some one imprisoned? – but a prisoner would surely not have had a lamp or have had access to the necessary materials. Could primitive man see better in the dark? This is a possible theory, but is not wholly satisfactory even if correct. A more probable explanation is to be found in the suggestion that the paintings had some magical significance, and that the caves were shrines. Were they perhaps totemic, representing the animals associated with particular tribes, whose prowess man sought to assimilate, or were they intended to aid the hunter with some form of sympathetic magic? Human figures are very rarely depicted, but in one case a man is shown dressed up as a deer, while in other caverns the position of the heart, the source of life, is clearly marked on the animals, and other beasts are shown with spears sticking into their sides (*Ill. 3*). The man dressed as a deer might well be a totemic figure, and the spears sticking into the beasts were meant to aid in their destruction – while the hunter was about his task in the forests

4 Left: outline drawing at La Mouthe, southern France. Three distinct techniques can be distinguished there; that of simple outline drawing would seem to be the earliest of them

5 Bison at Lascaux, southern France. Though the animals at Lascaux are perhaps less exact as naturalistic representations than those at Altamira (*Ills. 2, 8, 9*), the technique of decoration is more elaborate and at times takes on the character of polychrome painting

6 Above: frieze at Lascaux known as the shaft of the Dead Man. The animals are definitely meant to be seen together as one composition; the fact too that more than one colour is used makes this an especially elaborate work

outside, the medicine-man was endeavouring to help him in his shrine of mystery by drawing pictures of the quarry, weaving the appropriate spells, and puncturing its heart or piercing its representation with drawings of spears, so that the quarry might fall an easy victim.

Whatever the basic aim behind these pictures, however, the fact remains that the men who painted the animals on the roof of the cave at Altamira, not to mention a mass of others who worked elsewhere, at La Mouthe (*Ill. 4*) or Font de Gaume (*Ill. 10*) for instance, or those who did bison's heads at Lascaux (*Ill. 6*), were artists of considerable ability, with a developed understanding of many of the basic problems of representational art. And at Lascaux there was further elaboration, for here was attempted what is clearly a composition (*Ill.7*). There a hunter is depicted along with the animals, though the human is poorly enough drawn in comparison with the fauna. Only later at Cogul do humans appear in large numbers, but the work there is not nearly as good as that of earlier date.

7 Below: painting in black outline at Lascaux. Note how much more satisfactory the bison is than the man. The curious bird on the pole beneath him is perhaps a totemic symbol

8 Above: the dying bison, Altamira, Spain. This is one of the most startlingly impressive of all the paintings of the Palaeolithic age. The bison is dead, but the muscles still remain relaxed and one feels that at any moment it might give one last convulsive kick

9 Below: standing bison, Altamira, Spain. Once more the inner nature, the spirit and massive strength of the bison, is conveyed with quite astonishing penetration and clarity, seldom surpassed in art at any period

10 Font de Gaume, southern France; a horse in black outline against a background of stalactites. The work at Font de Gaume is perhaps not quite as accomplished as that at Altamira, but it is nevertheless original and unusual

THE TWENTY THOUSAND MISSING YEARS

Altamira, Lascaux and the other Palaeolithic caves are known to us by the astonishing luck of their survival. For the Neolithic Age, and the long struggle of early man towards civilization, there has been (so far) no corresponding revelation. Did the animal art just die out? Were the races to whom the artists belonged annihilated? Did Neolithic man never achieve comparable skills? We do not know. For these millennia we have stone implements and weapons but almost no representational art. From the objects that have survived we can gather something. They are often decorated with formal and geometric patterns, such as the repeating spiral. This occurs on much early pottery, on some rock carvings, such as those of New Grange in Ireland (*Ill. 11*) and doubtless on painted decoration also. It represents the opposite pole from the Palaeolithic animal art, so that already by this time we can recognize the two basic categories between which art was to oscillate thereafter – the abstract and the representational.

The problem of representation is to imitate or copy nature, that of creation to organize forms to produce a pleasing or significant pattern which does not exist in nature. Most art has attempted to combine the two, but some has confined itself to the second, and this art, basically one of abstraction, cannot be dismissed as mere craftsmanship, as some critics would suggest; all the manifestations of the last half century go to show that representation, though it has more often than not been the main trend that art has followed through the long ages of man's history, has nevertheless not been the only one; witness again the decoration of the early potteries of China, that of the Geometric phase of Greek art, or the illuminations in the manuscripts of the so-called Hiberno-Saxon school (*Ills. 85–92*).

Neolithic artists, however, were certainly not all formalists. Quite recently, in the course of some extremely important excavations in Asia Minor, a series of wall paintings has been unearthed on which hunting scenes of great vigour and spirit are depicted. Here, as in the art of the Bushmen and other tribes of Africa, the feeling for nature was far less developed than it was in Palaeolithic times; there was little attempt to express the three-dimensional; the animals are at best childish, at worst barely recognizable; the human figures are crude and wholly conventional; but the action is vivid, the theme clear and distinct. Here it is the subject-matter, the depiction of the scene, which is the factor that counts, not the pattern that the figures make on the wall surface; or their truth to nature. In all of these works animals, men and their various accoutrements are combined together in active association. The artist's aim was to tell a story in as dramatic a manner as possible, even if his figures were little more than symbols. So we see here at its earliest stage another of the elements that contributed to the make-up of later art, that of recording events. However, though primitive men had, in their different ways, solved independently the problems of representation, recording and creation, it was not until a much later age that all three approaches came to be blended in a single work.

By the early years of the second millennium BC the darkness is lifting. In the story that now begins there are no more gaps. It is a continuous stream, leading to and including the art of our own age.

11 Neolithic art. Spirals engraved on the rock, from the great megalithic tomb of New Grange in Ireland. Whereas Palaeolithic art was basically naturalistic, the art of Neolithic times was in the main non-representational, making use of formal designs and abstract patterns ▶

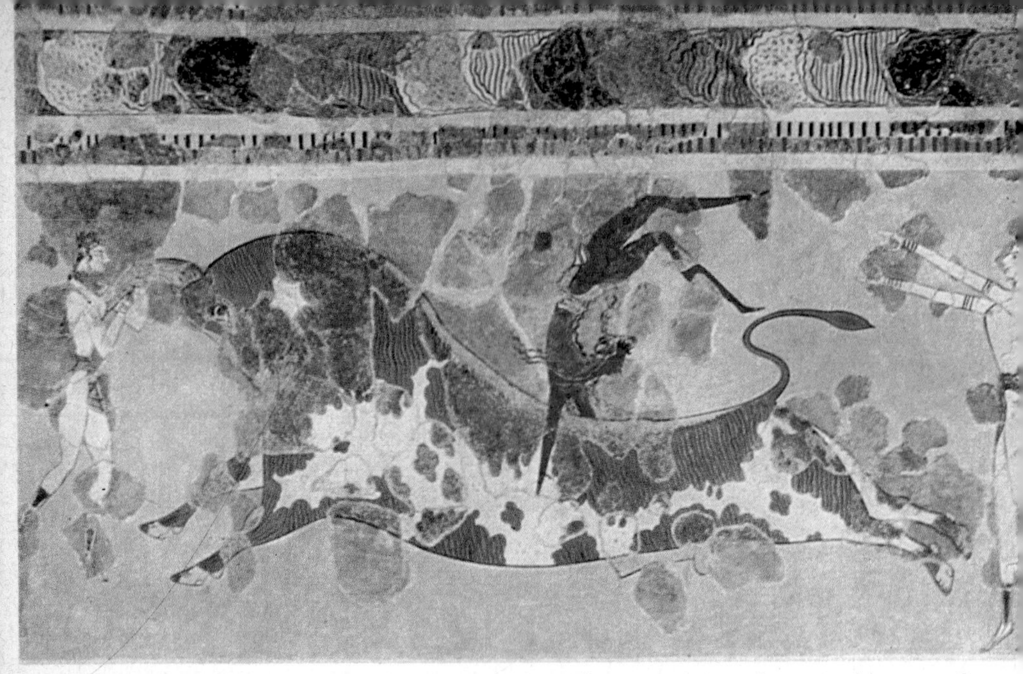

12 Above: wall paintings in the Palace of Knossos, Crete, depicting the game of bull-jumping. The athlete had to grasp the bull by its horns, turn a somersault on its back and then land on the ground behind

CHAPTER TWO

Minoan art: the bull-cult and the sea

European art begins outside Europe. To follow it back to its origins we should have to go laboriously through the findings of archaeologists in Egypt, Syria, Palestine and Mesopotamia – for it was here that Western civilization was born. To do this, however, would take us outside the scope of this book, introducing analogues, influences, connexions and parallels that would complicate our understanding without really enriching it. One has to begin somewhere, and there is nowhere better than the point at which painting first becomes truly European, that is, the Minoan Age in Crete.

No one knows where the Minoans came from or how their great sea-empire was built up. Their language (so it appears since the decipherment of the Linear B tablets) was an early form of Greek, their culture seems to have relied largely on that of Egypt and the Near East. But here, for the first time in Europe, are populous towns, settled agriculture, and vast royal palaces – a sophisticated way of life and a sophisticated art. The biggest of the palaces, that at Knossos, dating from the mid-second millennium BC, was excavated by Sir Arthur Evans. He found several wall paintings as notable for their skill and beauty as for their age and state of preservation (*Ills. 12, 15*). They were battered and broken it is true, but were well enough preserved to permit the restoration of at least some of the scenes. Frequently they depict the Cretan sport of bull jumping; others are connected with the cult of the minotaur; always human figures, bulls and marine and floral morifs dominate, done in bright colours against a blue background. The scenes show great spirit and liveliness, and are gay, brilliant and full of movement. In many cases, they are

13 A frieze of offering bearers, from Agia Triada. At the left-hand end are standards with the double-axe symbol at the top. The drawing of figures in profile was ◀ universal in Cretan art

of a semi-ritual character (*Ill. 13*), and the significance of some of the subject-matter is obscure to us today, but even if we cannot understand the true import of the scenes, we can nevertheless delight in their gay colours and flowing designs.

If I choose a single motif to characterize Minoan painting it will have to be a strange one – the octopus. It was easily the Cretan's favourite animal. It reflected his obvious love of the sea and its dynamic, twining tentacles were depicted not only with a great feeling for their ornamental possibilities, but also with a great understanding of the particular nature of the creature itself. If the Palaeolithic artist was able to render the innate characteristics of the bison with particular understanding, the Cretan artist was similarly competent at dealing with the octopus; somehow the renderings of these creatures on the pottery (*Ill. 14*) seem more convincing than the narrative paintings of the bulls and humans on the walls. But though they have a strange, doll-like quality, the Cretan women and their costumes, with wide, bell-like skirt below and bare breasts above, are delightful and particularly charming.

14 Pottery flask from Knossos with octopus ornament. The octopus motif was a great favourite of the Cretan potters, its sinuous lines and association with the sea making it uniquely representative of the great age of Minoan art

15 Detail of a figure from the Knossos wall paintings. The large eyes and long nose are typical of the features most favoured in Crete at the time. The style of beauty and perhaps the slightly provocative expression earned this the name of 'La Parisienne' – the Parisian girl – when it was first discovered ▶

CHAPTER THREE

Greece, Etruria and Rome

Imagine all the great works of Italian Renaissance painting – the Sistine Ceiling, the *Stanze* of Raphael, the Brancacci Chapel, the *Mona Lisa* – to have been destroyed. Imagine that while they had existed a few copies had been made, that the makers of plates, pitchers and souvenir mugs had also adopted them to their own wares, and that a few art lovers had written enthusiastic but vague descriptions of the pictures they particularly admired. Then imagine a historian with this material trying to write a balanced and meaningful history of Renaissance painting, and you have an idea of the sort of task facing anyone who sets out to write this chapter. It is true that the Greek vase painters were often considerable artists in their own right, offering a study as rewarding and enjoyable as any art of later times, but the great men – the men whom the Greeks themselves regarded as their leading painters – are mere names (Zeuxis, Apelles) and will always remain so. Of Etruscan painting very much more survives and gives us in some ways our most vivid insight into what Greek painting must have been like. Roman painting, too, is known in some quantity, though it is uneven in quality and that of Pompeii inevitably assumes an importance for us out of all proportion to its contemporary value.

GREEK PAINTING: REFLECTIONS OF GREATNESS

The earliest Greek vase painting looks back at Neolithic models (*Ill. 16*). The designs are geometric, the patterns make their effect by rhythm and balance and there is hardly a hint of representational forms (the only exception is some very stylized animal shapes). Indeed, the decoration is much more formal than that used centuries earlier in Crete.

16 Athenian krater, with ornament in the so-called geometric style. The krater was a simple, two-handled jar – in this case the lid is surmounted by a small jug. ◀ All the ornament is severely abstract except for the very stylized horses

17 Detail of the decoration of a krater from Argos. Here the non-representational ornament of the earlier phase is giving place to a figural one, though the figures remain stylized. The subject is Odysseus and his companions putting out the single eye of the giant Cyclops

This severe, non-representational style did not last for long. Very soon the idea of depiction was born – or born again – and almost at once, even when the actual depiction was not very efficient, drama and narrative began to play a very important role. A picture of the mid-seventh century BC on a krater from Argos shows this clearly enough (*Ill. 17*). It depicts the blinding of Polyphemus by Odysseus, and in spite of the narrow conventions of the art, illustrates the story with considerable force. Martin Robertson, in his book on Greek painting, suggests that it was inspired by a wall painting, for the theme is one which is obviously better suited to a rendering on a large scale. But it must have been drastically modified from its original. In the first place, the wall surface was flat, for curved constructions like domes and vaults were not known to the Greeks, and considerable distortions were necessary to adjust the figure on the flat walls to the curved surface of a vase, or vice versa; and in the second, though the vase paintings are of great beauty, they tell by the excellence of their detail rather than by the grandeur of their compositions, and all the evidence goes to show that the wall paintings were grand and monumental, even if great attention was given to naturalism and detail.

In the vases we can trace a gradual and fairly rapid evolution away from stylization and towards naturalism. The earliest phase, as we have seen, was almost wholly abstract; it is appropriately known as the 'Geometric'. In the next, which was not wholly indigenous to Greece, but stemmed from Asia, living forms had a considerable role to play, but they were stylized and as often as not fantastic rather than real, in spite of the accuracy of the detail, and tended to be treated as parts of a pattern rather than for themselves; often, for example, two identical monsters were shown confronted (*Ill. 18*). This is known as the orientalizing phase. The results are perhaps to be described as decorative rather than as fine art, but they are, none the less, often both impressive and delightful.

18 Vase from Kameiros, Rhodes, with decoration of the type known as Corinthian. The ornament, lions and a snake above, and two fantastic birds sharing a common head below, illustrates the oriental style which was strongly influencing Greek art at this time

In the next phase of vase painting, which is known as the 'Black Figure' style, the figures take the form of silhouettes in black against the natural red grounds of the pots (*Ill. 19*). Here the drawing is much more naturalistic, and considerable attention is paid to the story that the pictures tell. It is thus a narrative as well as a pictorial art, and the style is dramatic, illustrative and forceful, being close in spirit to that of the Greek drama. Athens was the main centre of its development and it was there that the finest vases of the age were made and painted. The forms of the vessels were very diverse and often very elaborate, the pottery fine and very thin, and the painting fired on as a kind of glaze, so that it is virtually as indestructible as the pottery itself. The clear-cut lines of the drawing and the spirited nature of the designs mark out the vases as affording one of the most complete expressions of the Greek artistic genius. We know the names not only of some of the potters, who were themselves revered for their great mastery of the craft, but also of the painters; of these Exekias and Nearchos were the most important.

With the sixth century BC, and still more with the fifth, coinciding with the upheavals of the Persian Wars, the technique underwent a reversal; the grounds were coloured black and the figures left in reserve, in the manner known as 'Red Figure'. It was here, perhaps, that the finest results of vase painting were produced, at the hands of men, some known by name, like Polygnotus, and some anonymous, though many of them boasted a very personal style. We can indeed often recognize the individual painter's work, and fictitious names have therefore been given to them by scholars; the so-called 'Berlin' and 'Brygos' painters were two of the greatest of them and their work is distinguished by a mastery of drawing, a precision of detail and a command of expression which has seldom been surpassed at any phase of art's development (*Ill. 21*). These men, and a few others, set the standard in Athens. Elsewhere their style was emulated, often with great success. But with mass production – and a vast mass of pottery was produced – there was a tendency to monotony, and much of the provincial work, though interesting to archaeologists, is somewhat depressing in the mass. To the non-specialist the vase galleries of a large museum are, to say the least,

19 The murder of Penthesilea by Achilles – a Homeric theme used in the decoration of an Athenian amphora. It is in the Black Figure technique, the figures standing out silhouetted against the red ground of the pot. This technique was the most usual one till the fifth century BC

daunting, but the sheer beauty of the draughtsmanship in the best work cannot be surpassed in the products of any age.

How much (allowing for differences in convention and medium) can we infer from these vases about the large-scale paintings?

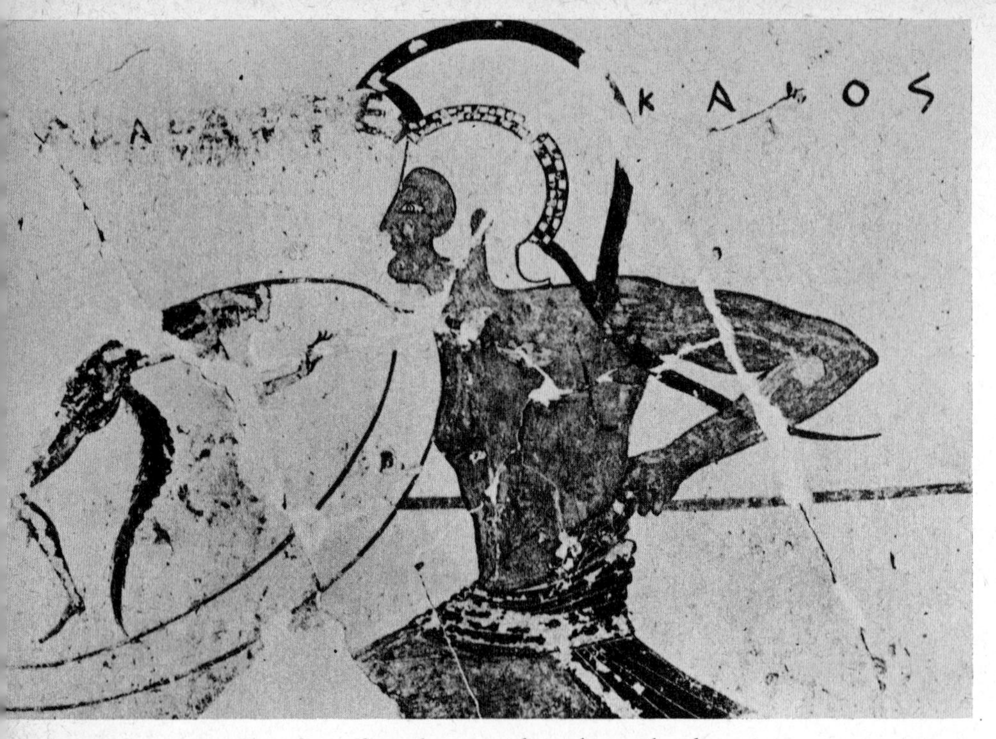

20 Clay plaque from the Acropolis, Athens. The plaque is important as it is one of the very few of the paintings of the sixth century BC other than vase paintings that have come down to us

Sometimes, as we have seen, we can guess that a vase has been copied from a flat picture (as when a composition is used which hardly makes sense on the curved surface – e.g. when a figure at the bottom is awkwardly twisted to fit a cramped space); sometimes a vase painting approximates to the written description of a fresco; and very occasionally a precious fragment of fresco has come to light to provide a direct comparison. One such fragment, part of a plaque of the late sixth century recovered from the Acropolis, is reproduced here (*Ill. 20*). It shows that, whatever may have been the similarities, the larger works must have been characterized by a rather freer style.

It is however the vases of the final phase that may be most effectively compared to large-scale works, for there the ground of the pot was coloured white like a canvas or a wall (*Ills. 22, 23*), and the decoration was drawn upon this ground in black or occasionally in

21 Detail of the decoration of an Athenian amphora in the Red Figure technique, showing Hermes and a satyr. Not only did the techniques of vase decoration change as time went forward, but also the style, which became progressively more naturalistic

other colours also. This is known as the 'White Ground' style and it existed alongside the others, though it was most in vogue during the fifth century BC. For a time the technique was used on vases of varying form, notably on the insides of cups, but it was most frequently employed to adorn the tall, thin vessels shaped like long-necked bottles with a handle at one side, known as 'Lekythoi', which were used at the funeral to contain sweet-smelling unguents. The scenes depicted on them are thus usually of a funerary character. The white grounds were prone to flake however, so that the drawings have often perished; in such cases forgers have redone them, and though the pots are mostly genuine, the drawings are often forgeries. Earlier in the fifth century the drawings on this White Ground style were forceful and vigorous, like those on a krater in the Vatican of *c.* 480 BC: later, *c.* 400 BC, they tended to prettiness; but always the work was characterized by an amazing economy of

22 Detail of lekythos from Athens, with decoration by the Phiale Painter. The work is in the White Ground technique characterized by very delicate, refined drawings in thin outline. It shows, with a most delicate pathos, an Athenian woman bringing offerings to her husband's tomb. The tall, thin vases on which this style of painting is normally found were used to hold unguents at funerals

23 Cup with decoration in the White Ground style – Aphrodite riding on a goose

line and they have both dignity and charm; a vase at Munich showing a woman seated at her husband's tomb is outstanding (*Ill. 22*). It was this style that inspired one of the numerous – and in many ways one of the most satisfactory – styles of Picasso's varied developments.

Together with Greek art we should include that of the numerous colonies and daughter-cities established outside Greece. An area of particular interest in the context of vase painting was south Italy or 'Magna Graecia'. The vases made here are unusual in showing a large number of comic scenes. They were no doubt inspired by the drama, and the figures that adorn them have something in common with those in some of the Pompeiian paintings which appear to represent actors. They are not very beautiful, but are interesting as representing

24 A miser being dragged off his money chest by thieves, from a vase found at Nola in southern Italy. Greek vases were exported in large numbers to Italy, those with scenes inspired by the comic drama being especially popular. Note how the characters wear masks, like actors

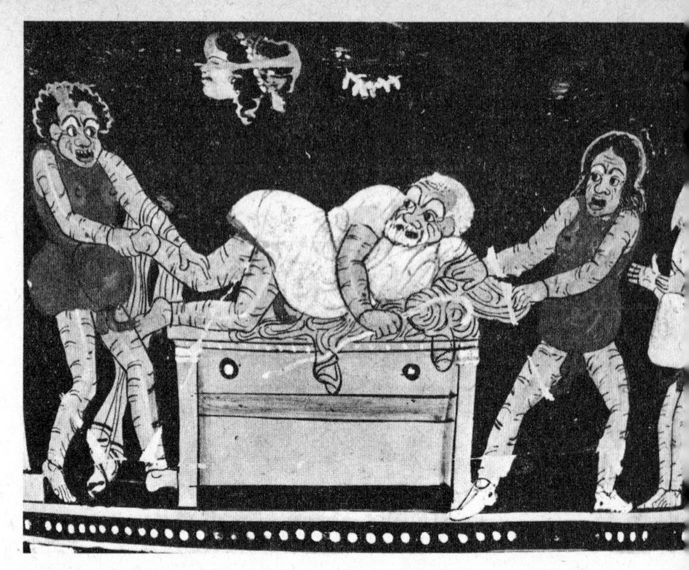

25 Darius of Persia turning to flee from the victorious Alexander. The subject was a very popular one from the time of Alexander onwards; indeed it was one of the favourite subjects of Hellenistic art. This mosaic, which is in the Museum at Naples, is really a Roman work in the Hellenistic style

26 Mosaic depicting a stag hunt from Alexander's capital at Pella near Salonica. It is made of small, carefully selected pebbles. The colours are thus limited to black and white, but the skill of the artist was such that the limitations of the material were completely overcome

an aspect of the Greek approach to art which is sometimes forgotten, namely a love of the grotesque (*Ill. 24*).

In so far as we can tell, the large-scale paintings produced on the Greek mainland, more especially those done in Athens, always tended towards the ideal; proportion, balance, beauty were the main preoccupations that governed the artists. In the provinces on the other hand, and more especially in the Greek lands of Asia Minor, with their great cities like Ephesus and Pergamon, a more dramatic style was developed which aimed on the one hand at making art more dynamic and on the other at introducing a greater degree of emotion. This is the style which we know as 'Hellenistic' and it developed from the end of the fourth century BC onwards. One of the most famous works of the age was a painting depicting Alexander's victory over Darius, a large composition, crowded with realistic and dramatic detail. It is known to us through a copy done in mosaic which is now in the museum at Naples (*Ill. 25*), but the same scene was no doubt reproduced on numerous occasions elsewhere.

For many years we depended almost entirely on such Roman copies for our knowledge of those Hellenistic paintings, but recently some very fine actual works have been unearthed, in the form of a series of mosaic floors from the site of Alexander's capital at Pella, situated near Salonica in northern Greece (*Ill. 26*). These mosaics are made of black and white pebbles, obviously a very restrictive medium, but the work is so skilled, the designs so proficient, that the results constitute works of art of very great beauty. Perhaps the high quality was to some extent due to the severe discipline that the use of such a limited material entailed.

With the progress of the Hellenistic period our knowledge of the painterly arts becomes more extensive, for in addition to these mosaics a few wall paintings are actually preserved, notably the decoration of a domed chamber at Kazanlik in Bulgaria (*Ill. 27*) and a number of paintings on walls from Hellenistic sites in the region of Olbia in south Russia; most important is that known as the *kurgan* of the Great Bliznitsa. The Bulgarian work is colourful but essentially provincial; that in Russia is of finer quality, but the style is distinct from that which dominated in Greece, for the search for expression has been carried very much further, and elegance has been sacrificed in favour of significance. Indeed, we see here for the first time the influence of a distinct type of art, which was to make itself very actively felt in the Early Christian period.

This trend was first developed in the lands to the east of the Mediterranean, and it was responsible for the more dramatic manner that distinguished the art of Asia Minor from that of Greece in the fourth century, but its full effect was only felt rather later, when it was developed by peoples of orientalizing character like the Parthians. The style travelled to the West along with the mystic Oriental religions like Gnosticism and Mithraism which became immensely popular throughout the Roman Empire at the beginning of the Christian era. We will have more to say of this expressionistic style later when we come to deal with the Early Christian period. In the south Russian paintings the influence of this orientalizing style is to be seen in the large staring eyes, the clumsy yet expressive faces and the frontal poses of the figures. Everything is less elegant, less refined, but at the same time more forceful, more dominating, than it would have been in Greece itself. These Russian finds were very fully published early in this century, but in recent years they have tended to be forgotten.

After the lightning conquests of Alexander the cultural centre of the Mediterranean world moved from Athens to Alexandria. Contemporary writers make many references to Alexandrian painting, but virtually nothing survives in the city. However, certain themes

27 The Hellenistic phase in art covered the last three centuries BC and was characterized by a realistic style which depended for its appeal mainly on drama. Sometimes, however, the elegance and beauty of Greece survived, as in the very fine paintings of the tomb chamber at Kazanlik in Bulgaria, which was discovered by chance only a few years ago

28 Above: a scene from the Nile, forming part of a Pompeiian mosaic floor. These 'Nilotic' subjects, which were extremely popular in Roman art, are yet another proof of the influence exercised in Italy by Hellenistic – in this case Alexandrian – art

29 Below: the wooden 'skene' of a Greek theatre, from a vase. Scenes like these led to such highly elaborate 'architecturescapes' as *Ill. 44*

30 Part of a fresco from Stabiae showing a Roman harbour scene. The painting belongs to the first century AD and is a fine example of the impressionistic technique evolved by Roman artists

which appear in mosaic floors from Africa to Britain and from Spain to Syria, as well as in the wall paintings of Pompeii and elsewhere, certainly stemmed from there. Depictions of crocodile hunts and scenes enacted in river swamps which are clearly Nilotic are the most important (*Ill. 28*). But to assign to Alexandria the whole initiative for the development of a new style of picturesque landscape painting

31 Romantic landscape from the villa of Agrippa Posthumus near Pompeii. The Pompeiian paintings cover a very wide range of subjects. The landscapes are mostly extremely modern in character, showing a real delight in country scenes for their own sake

which became popular throughout the Roman world in the second century BC, as some scholars tend to do, is to exaggerate unduly. The Nilotic scenes no doubt came from Egypt, but a love for landscape and country scenes certainly developed at an early date in Italy, while the interest in architectural backgrounds, which is a distinctive feature of Roman paintings as a whole, may well have first developed in Greece, inspired, perhaps, by the idea of depicting theatre settings – a fragment of a vase from Tarentum shows such a motif (*Ill. 29*).

Wherever the style originated, however, a love of landscapes and of what may best be termed architecturescapes, developed all over Italy during the second and first centuries (*Ill. 30*). There are numerous examples at Pompeii, and similar themes would appear to have formed the basis of painting throughout the Roman world, so that they became distinctive of Roman art; classical compositions which continued to be very popular on the other hand represent the Greek contribution. Most of them were more or less straight copies of Greek paintings (*Ill. 32*), just as marbles like the various well-known figures of Venus are Roman copies of Greek sculptures. According to Pliny the Elder the landscapes were invented by Ludius at the time of Augustus, but in actual fact they go back to a much earlier date, and those where classical scenes are set in landscape surroundings, like the wall painting from the Villa of Agrippa Posthumus near Pompeii (*Ill. 31*), may well be free copies of Greek originals. But in the Greek original the story no doubt played a larger part than in the Roman version, where the landscape itself was stressed.

32 The Three Graces – a very popular classical group seen here in a fresco from Pompeii. Since being rediscovered by the Renaissance, the subject has inspired many great artists from Raphael to Kokoschka

THE ETRUSCANS: ART FOR THE DEAD

Greek art spread all over the Mediterranean, from Spain to the Crimea and from Marseilles to Alexandria. Its course in central Italy, however, is of special interest. Firstly it can be followed from the very earliest phases of Greek culture (the so-called 'Archaic' period); secondly it has survived on a scale to which there is no parallel in Greece itself; thirdly it was this art – Etruscan art – which gave birth to that of Rome.

Who the Etruscans were is perhaps the knottiest problem in classical archaeology. In this context it is sufficient to say that their culture was dominated by Greece. They imported Greek works of art wholesale; their own pottery, metalwork and (we presume) wall paintings were all based on Greek examples; and although they spoke a totally different language they borrowed the Greek alphabet to write it down.

The Etruscans obviously loved painting and surrounded themselves with it in their lives. In the tombs for their dead (for whose care

33 Left: painting from the tomb of the Leopards at Tarquinia, *c.* 470 BC; though the art of the Etruscans owed a considerable debt to Greece the style is nevertheless distinct. Here we see the banquet of the dead – the joys of this life projected into the next

34 Below: part of a frieze from Tarquinia showing a youth on horseback. The Etruscan artists inherited from Egypt the habit of turning the shoulders full-face in a sideways view, but in spite of these and other conventions, they were able to give a brilliant vividness to their figures, especially the animals

35 The Etruscan paintings that have come down to us all come from tombs. Here a man and his wife take part in a funeral feast. In this work, which comes late in the Etruscan period, there is a touch of sadness, absent in the joyful earlier paintings

they had an obsessive concern) they built replica houses complete with furniture, pottery – and frescoes. It is these which have survived in such abundance and which make the Etruscans as alive for us, although they left no literature, as any other people in history. The tombs took the form of largish chambers carved out of the rock below the ground. Their walls were adorned with paintings, sometimes on plaster, sometimes on the rock face itself, and when the burial had been completed the tombs were firmly and carefully sealed. This assured the preservation of the paintings, and as the tombs were below ground-level they often escaped the attention of tomb robbers. When first opened the colours of these tomb paintings are as fresh as on the day on which they were executed. Unfortunately, they tend to fade very rapidly and those which were discovered during the nineteenth century, or even early in the twentieth, have either perished or survive as little more than colourless ghosts. But in recent times methods of conservation have been perfected, and now the paintings can also be photographed through a small aperture in the roof before the tomb is actually opened.

Apart from the variety and brilliance of their colours these paintings make their effect by the delightful rhythms of their composition. Scenes of hunting and fishing, various athletic activities and banquets (*Ill. 33*) form the most popular subject-matter, the former to make sure that the deceased could enjoy in the after-life what he had enjoyed on earth, the banquets to make sure that he should never be short of food. The figures are invariably shown in profile, and although there is a tendency to swing the shoulders round so that both of them are visible, as in Egyptian painting, the rigid conventions of Egyptian art were avoided, and the figures are vivid and active. The prancing horses, with long flowing tails, are especially attractive (*Ill. 34*).

The earliest work dates from the sixth century BC. Greek ideas exercised a powerful influence, yet the art is not a Greek art – it has a strikingly individual character, more forceful and more angular on the one hand, less elegant, perhaps even cruder, on the other. Death, often of a cruel and violent type, as in portrayals of the slaughter of prisoners, had no horrors for the Etruscans, in any case in early times. With the fourth century, episodes from Greek mythology began to play a more important role, but the Etruscans, in the tomb paintings, continued to prefer themes connected with the underworld and Greek ideas were not wholly accepted by them. Indeed, as time went on they tended to develop a rather gloomy attitude in opposition to the gaiety that was such an essential of the Greek outlook, and threatening demons began to play an important role in the iconography. The calm acceptance of death so characteristic of the earlier phases gave way in the banquet scenes to a more melancholy attitude, where regrets for the life that is being left behind begin to be more dominant (*Ill. 35*). But some later paintings are very impressive, notably one from the tomb of Typhon at Tarquinia, dating probably from the first century BC, where great giants hold up the heavens. It is possessed of a monumental grandeur which is wholly distinctive, and really marks the end of the Etruscan phase; official Roman art which followed it was to be much more concerned with the recording of events, to the glorification of the Caesar or the Roman people.

36 Wall painting, the Garden of Livia in Rome. These large landscapes are often of outstanding beauty and from the purely artistic point of view constitute the most important development of all Roman painting

ROME: ART FOR AN EMPIRE

Roman art represents a fusion between Hellenistic art (itself a rich amalgam of styles) and that of the Etruscans. But from a quite early date (second century BC) a distinct style of decoration emerges in which secular subjects are beginning to predominate over religious ones. Naturally, the miraculous survival of Pompeii, and of the neighbouring towns Herculaneum and Stabiae, colours all our ideas about Roman painting. Covered by solid volcanic dust from the famous eruption of Vesuvius in AD 79, buildings have been preserved in superb condition often to the height of two storeys. Practically every house, from the poorest to the grandest, seems to have possessed some sort of decoration, either painted or in mosaic, and the work was mostly of a very high quality.

In the more important houses, scenes drawn from Greek mythology were especially popular (*Ills. 32, 38*); most of them were copies

37 Below: still life with basket of fruits from the house of Julia Felix, Pompeii. This is a wall painting, but the texts speak also of portable pictures, which must often have been very like this

38 Left: Perseus and Andromeda from the house of Dioscorides, Pompeii. This stately composition is probably just as close to its Greek original as one of the Roman copies of a Greek statue

of Greek originals, and there is reason to believe that the copies were very faithful. The choice between scenes of a grandiose nature and those of a lighter character was no doubt dictated by the tastes of the owners, though the great popularity which Venus enjoyed was due not only to the attraction she exercised as goddess of love and beauty, but also to the fact that she was the patron goddess of Pompeii. The numerous theatre scenes (*Ill. 40*) also owed a debt to Greece, for they often depicted classical plays. But more realist subjects, such as portraits of theatrical personalities or depictions of rehearsals being conducted, often by comic actors, were more truly Roman in spirit. A famous mosaic showing dancers and a man with a tambourine belongs to this group; it probably depicts a company of strolling players (*Ill. 39*). Genre scenes were especially popular and were invariably rendered with considerable realism, and here again Roman rather than Greek tastes are reflected. Those which depicted events from everyday life were often extremely vivid.

39 Mosaic showing strolling players, from Pompeii. These mosaics, using cubes of glass as well as stone, were the first to be placed vertically on walls or in niches, rather than flat on the floor

40 Wall painting from Herculaneum depicting a tragic actor. Once more the style is more Greek than Roman, and there has been a clear search for dignity and beauty

Realist again were the still-lifes, where the local foodstuffs both animal and vegetable, formed the subject-matter. Many of them were intended as shop signs, but even so great skill in composition as well as in actual depiction made these works of art of very considerable quality (*Ill. 37*). The examples we know are all wall paintings, but Pliny refers to a sale of pictures, so no doubt panels were also produced; they would perhaps have been destroyed by the hot ashes of the eruption of Vesuvius whereas the walls remained unaffected.

We have seen how landscape painting probably originated with the school of Alexandria. Roman artists carried it to a new level of refinement. Pictures of birds alone or birds in trees were also popular and accorded well with the Roman love of landscape for its own sake. Birds and trees often played a part in delightful garden scenes, where great skill was manifested in the rendering of light and shade. These garden scenes are often enchanting (*Ill. 36*), many of them would not

41 Probably the most famous of all Roman paintings (because discovered as early as the sixteenth century) is the so-called 'Aldobrandini Wedding' painted on the wall of a mansion in Rome. This detail shows the bride, on the right, being consoled by the goddess Aphrodite. On the left another woman, perhaps the bride's mother, dips her hand in a basin. The work is close to the Pompeiian second style, and shows considerable understanding of depth and modelling

seem out of place in an exhibition of seventeenth-century paintings for they show the same predominant delight in the charms of nature.

Such works were often meant to be seen not on their own but as part of larger decorative schemes, covering whole walls or even rooms. At Pompeii four phases or 'styles' have been distinguished. In the first, rows of pillars partitioned the walls; there were no figures and the rendering of perspective was elementary. In the second, the

architecture was more imaginative and deep perspective vistas formed an essential part of each composition. Mythological scenes seem to have been in special favour at this time as the principal themes for the subject-matter included within the architectural framing; a Roman picture called the *Aldobrandini Wedding* is typical (*Ill. 41*).

In paintings of what is called the third style, greater stress was laid on ornament. Mythological scenes went out of fashion and the deep perspectives of the second style were discarded in favour of rather flatter compositions made up of tall, thin columns, essentially decorative in conception. The colours became gayer and lighter, and the general effect more imaginative. Finally, in the last phase, which was developed during the last thirty years before the destruction of Pompeii in AD 79, the walls were treated like theatre scenery and vast perspective views of Baroque character were conceived (*Ill. 44*). They resemble, often enough, the work of the great theatre designers of seventeenth-century Italy, as, for example, that of the Bibienas.

But perhaps Rome's greatest single contribution to the art of painting – as of sculpture – lies in the sphere of portraiture. No painting seen so far in this book could be called a portrait, but the Romans left us scores of vivid likenesses of real men and women (*Ill. 43*), varying from tradespeople (on wooden signs set up over their shops) to lords and emperors. Fashionable portraiture, as we know from survivals at Pompeii, had reached a pitch of great sophistication and charm, but a more severe, more expressive style was in being elsewhere, and was to a great extent under the influence of the expressive oriental style we noted when discussing Hellenistic painting in south Russia. In the years around the birth of Christ this more expressive style is to be seen in the panels done as mummy portraits in Egypt (*Ill. 42*). They were executed on boards, sometimes in a sort of tempera, sometimes in the encaustic technique, where the medium for the colours was wax. The panels were set in the wrappings above the face of the deceased before burial; they took the place in fact of the more conventional mummy case that had been in use in ancient Egypt over countless centuries. Some of these portraits were no doubt stock products, reproducing conventional types, such as older men with beards, young men clean-shaven, and so on; but others were characterful, realistic portraits, in which the artist obviously set out to convey not so much the charm of the individual as the sterner, more profound aspects of his make-up which were more in keeping with his life in the world to come. The eyes were thus deep-set and contemplative, the colours sombre, the expressions intense, and it is not surprising that Christian patrons, as soon as they were able to exercise a choice, turned to this art rather than to the gayer, more artificial style that was popular at Pompeii.

42 An Egypto-Roman mummy portrait in the encaustic technique, from the Fayum near Cairo. These portraits were made to bind in the wrappings above the face of the deceased. Some were stock portraits of young women, older men and so on, but others were clearly done from life and are works of very high quality ▶

43 Left: portraits of Terentius Neo and his wife. The sensitive and realistic portraits form an important aspect of Pompeiian painting. Some were used as shop signs and presumably depicted the proprietors of the shop

44 Opposite: as time went on the architectural decorations on the walls of the Pompeiian houses became more and more baroque in style; works of the final phase, dating from shortly before the destruction of the city in A D 79, resemble Italian theatre decorations of the seventeenth century ▶

At one time this severe style was set aside by critics with the comment that it was merely the result of decadence. More recently however a fuller understanding of the problems of art history has resulted in the acceptance of the existence of an independent 'expressionist' style, and there is reason to believe that in this case the manner was first developed in Syria or perhaps even farther to the East, in the centuries immediately preceding the birth of Christ. Certain elements that characterize the style have even been associated with the Parthians, while others are to the fore in the art of Palmyra, an independent orientalizing city in the desert between Syria and Mesopotamia, on the extreme fringe of the Roman Empire. But many of the salient features, such as the frontal pose, the large staring eyes, and the search for inner significance, were particularly well suited to the ideas of the early Christians, and it was under the patronage of the new faith that the manner grew to prominence.

45 Head of an Apostle – a fragment of Early Christian painting from the Hypogeum of the Aurelians. The affinities with pagan Roman art are very clear, and the quality proves that the Christian community included trained professional artists

CHAPTER FOUR

The impact of Christianity

We saw in the last chapter how a change in style was enabling artists to give deeper and more tragic overtones to their paintings, especially portraits. It is tempting to discover in these stylistic developments symptoms of a spiritual change, and to equate this with the psychological mood of the third and fourth centuries AD, when Christianity was making its decisive large-scale conversions. Tempting but misleading. That there can be no such easy correlation between religious belief and artistic styles is evident from the fact that the first examples of the new style come in non-Christian contexts and that the first Christian art is not in this style.

Christianity was officially tolerated in 313. Before that all our evidence comes from the catacombs, underground burial galleries cut in the rock outside Rome and other cities. Often the paintings done here are crude enough, the work of men of no great talent, albeit wholly sincere; but others, even in their present battered state, prove that artists of real ability belonged to the Christian community, or at least worked for Christian patrons.

In style, however, and often – to all appearance – in subject-matter, they do not differ from contemporary pagan works. The early Christians hid their own doctrines under ambiguous motifs which would raise no comment among outsiders. A basket of food, or a loaf of bread thus symbolized the Eucharist, a dove the Peace of the Church, a peacock the Resurrection or a fish the name of Christ. Even explicit pagan themes are used, with new meanings. Garlands, birds and architectural motifs close to those in houses at Pompeii are extremely common, though instead of being purely decorative, they have a symbolic significance. Scenes of the countryside thus represent Paradise; a figure which would seem to depict Orpheus with animals around him is in reality Christ with his disciples (*Ill. 47*); figures of Eros, which seem wholly pagan, have taken on a Christian character and foreshadow the cherubs of Renaissance church art.

Certain other themes, however, are more obviously Christian, and depict events from the Old and New Testaments in a realistic manner. The scene of Moses striking the rock with his rod (*Ill. 48*) thus appears in the Catacomb of Callixtus, that of the Three Hebrews in the Fiery Furnace in the Catacomb of Priscilla (*Ill. 49*), while events from the New Testament, like the Last Supper, were quite frequently illustrated. Both the Last Supper and the Marriage at Cana were especially popular themes, for they symbolized the idea of the Eucharist, the central feast of the Christian faith. The former was depicted both in a fully representational manner showing Christ and the Apostles seated on couches behind a semicircular table, or symbolically, in the form of a basket and some loaves or fish, which served to embody the underlying idea. The scene where Balaam points out the star to Mary in the Catacomb of Priscilla (*Ill. 46*) – perhaps the earliest rendering of the Virgin and Child in Christian art – or the head of an Apostle in the Hypogeum of Aurelius (*Ill. 45*) are both works of real quality. In both, the naturalism and beauty of the classical trend in art is easy to recognize; they may be contrasted with the more forceful, more expressive rendering of the Virgin in the Cemetery of Maius, where the expressive oriental heritage dominates.

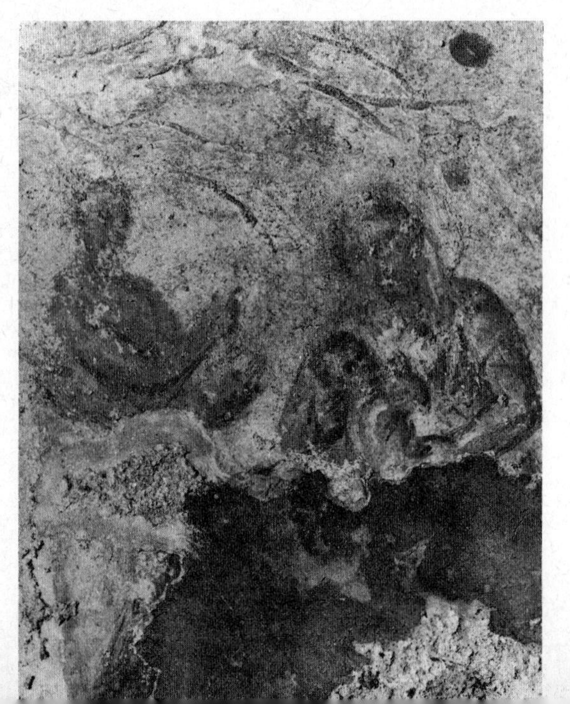

46 Balaam points out the star to Mary, from the Catacomb of Priscilla, Rome. This is probably the earliest depiction of the Virgin and Child known to us in Christian art

47 Jesus as the Good Shepherd: a painting from the Catacomb of Domitilla, Rome. The principal figure represents Christ, but it is modelled on a classical prototype, Orpheus. Early Christian art drew extensively from pagan models of this type; a truly Christian iconography really only developed in the fifth century

48 Painting from the Catacomb of Callixtus – Moses striking the Rock. An Old Testament iconography was developed earlier than that of the New; many of the scenes had probably been depicted before Christian times

49 Painting from the Catacomb of Priscilla, the Three Hebrews in the Fiery Furnace. This was a very popular theme in Early Christian art, symbolizing the idea of Resurrection

50 Mosaic floor from the great palace of the Byzantine emperors at Constantinople. Scenes of country life are shown with a great feeling for naturalism, but by the time this floor was laid – probably the later sixth century – such realistic details as shadows and the ground on which the figures stood were omitted

PAINTING IN STONE

The art which was to become most characteristic of the early Christians, and of the Byzantines who followed them in the East, was mosaic. Its origins can be traced back several centuries before the Age of Constantine. We have seen how a black and white pebble mosaic had been used at Alexander's palace of Pella. By the first century AD cubes of coloured marble have replaced the pebbles and already at Pompeii are employed with considerable effect to decorate niches or small wall-panels.

Why, it may be asked, should mosaic be included in a history of painting? Because the two arts run parallel, the same men often worked in both materials following the same conventions, often using the same designs, and aiming largely at the same effects. It would therefore be pedantic to attempt a radical separation. Indeed, the first masterpiece of Hellenistic mosaic to have come down to us is a copy of a painting – Alexander's victory over Darius seen in *Ill. 25*. This was made for a rich art lover at Pompeii. It consists of small pieces of coloured stone and forms the pavement of a room. During the early years of the Christian era such floor mosaics were more or less essential parts of every prosperous house or villa from Britain to Syria and from Gaul to North Africa. At first the scenes were depicted with great realism; the ground on which the figures stood was clearly indicated, the figures themselves cast shadows; animals, trees, rocks and so forth were rendered naturalistically, and the human beings were elegant and dynamic, like those of classical sculpture; great efforts were made to convey an impression of three-dimensional depth. As time went on, however, a new, more imaginative approach developed; the ground ceased to be shown, so that the figures seemed poised in space; cast shadows were omitted, so that the figures lost reality; rocks tended to become conventionalized as pieces of 'significant form', and the pictures became much flatter and more two-dimensional. Large numbers of these floors are preserved in North Africa (*Ills. 52, 53*), where they seem to have been

51 Girls in bikinis playing a ball game – part of a mosaic floor from Piazza Armerina in Sicily; probably to be dated to about AD 400. The whole floor covers a very large area and comprises a mass of hunting and other lively scenes

52, 53 Two details from a floor mosaic from Tripolitania: a scroll taking on the form of a bird's nest, and a threshing scene. There is a real feeling for nature and a greater degree of realism than appears later in the mosaics of the great palace

especially popular, and a whole series from the third to the sixth century has been unearthed at Antioch; these are especially interesting, for they show the progress of stylistic change over the centuries in a single centre. Taken as a whole the earlier ones are much more proficient than the later, but the changes that took place are not wholly to be attributed to decadence, but also to the penetration into art as a whole of anti-naturalistic ideas.

The process of evolution had progressed very far by the time that the magnificent floor of a section of the Great Palace of the Byzantine Emperors at Constantinople was laid, probably soon after the middle of the sixth century. It occupied four sides of a great court, some seventy yards long and ten deep, and was made up of a number of isolated compositions, such as hunting scenes, gladiatorial combats, children's games or agricultural and other country activities (*Ill. 50*). All are shown with great realism and panache, and at first glance they seem to be essentially classical in spirit (*Ill. 54*). But on closer examination a clear departure from classical canons becomes apparent, for the ground is seldom included, there is no attempt to indicate depth, and the figures appear to be floating in space before the plain backgrounds. This change was not in any way due to lack of skill, for the Constantinople floor has never been surpassed in quality from the technical point of view. Rather do we see here the influence of a new outlook in art which was making itself felt at the time. The change is most clearly apparent in religious art, where new themes and new ideas were being developed; here we see it in secular art, where the classical subject-matter survives though it is treated in a manner which heralds that of the Middle Ages.

In Christian art of course the change was impelled by the teachings of the new faith, which sought to stress the value of a spiritual, unworldly outlook as against a materialistic one. Just as in Christian teaching the inner workings of the soul were counted as of greater import than the claims of the flesh, so in art the meaning, the

54 Head from the mosaic floor of the great palace at Constantinople (*Ill. 50*). In spite of the fact that the head forms part of a decorative scroll, it is still treated with great realism and has the appearance of being done from life; it might depict a Goth

message, was more significant than any charm or beauty of the surface; similarly in architecture the exterior of the building counted for little, whereas the interior was profusely and richly decorated, to make it a worthy home for the living God.

It is just this change which we have already noted in portraiture, and which was clearly not simply the result of Christian teaching. We saw that it stemmed from the Near East and especially from Syria. In any case it is there that the most impressive and characteristic example of the style survives, namely the famous painting of a religious ceremony from the Temple of the Palmyrene gods at Dura, done *c.* AD 85 under Parthian patronage (*Ill.* 55). The figures are posed frontally, the conception is two-dimensional, and the work has a strange, mystic character which makes it extremely impressive. Hinks once termed this the 'levitating style', for the figures seem to be suspended in space rather than firmly planted on the ground, and their whole essence is spiritual rather than material. It is a very impressive painting, and must have been the work of a master of considerable ability, but it is perhaps most important because it is the earliest large-scale painting in the orientalizing manner that has survived. It was to boast many successors, and it is not without reason that Breasted, who first published it, called it an 'oriental forerunner of Byzantine painting'.

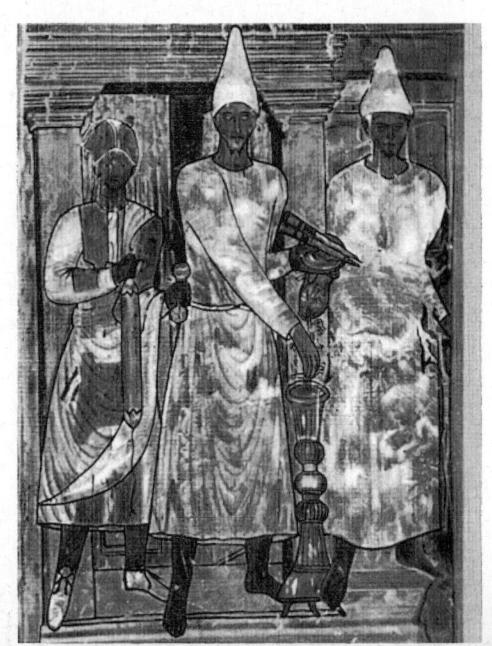

55 Painting of a ritual scene on the wall of the Temple of the Palmyrene gods at Dura in northern Syria, AD 85. The painting is characterized by the frontal poses, the rigid attitudes and the 'levitating' treatment, the figures seeming to float above the ground instead of standing on it

56 Procession of female saints – wall mosaic done in about 561 for the church of S. Apollinare Nuovo at Ravenna. The varied repetition of the figures is so skilful that they do not seem monotonous, but rather convey an effect of dignified movement as in a ritual dance

PAINTING IN LIGHT

By the Age of Justinian (mid-sixth century) this style – frontal, hieratic, impassive as it seemed – blended with that inherited from the classical world to produce a new art, the art we know as Byzantine. This was already a sophisticated art that was capable of producing virtually any effect it chose, from imperial grandeur to austere humility, from the awe-inspiring terror of Christ in Judgment to the tenderness of young girl-saints and the charm of little animals and birds. There had also been a vital change in material and technique. Instead of stone the Byzantine mosaicists began to use cubes of coloured glass – a rich glowing medium that never lost its brilliance and which made the walls of their churches alive with light. For it was upon the walls and vaults, not the floors, that they now lavished their genius. The imperial city of Ravenna, the Emperor's headquarters in Italy, still contains a series of over half a dozen churches or chapels which preserve all or part of their original mosaic decoration.

57 Mosaic from Sta Costanza, Rome, early fourth century. Though it adorns one of the vaults, the style is still very like that of a floor mosaic and the wholly classical heritage is clearly evident

Most famous of all are the two portrait groups of Justinian and Theodora in S. Vitale (second quarter of the sixth century), superb evocations of Byzantine court ceremonial (*Ill. 58*). Of roughly the same date and of similar character is the Procession of Saints in S. Apollinare Nuovo (*Ill. 56*). In both these works there is the same love of formality, the same stress on the unworldly, and in both, though especially in the latter, rhythm has begun to play a new and more important role. At the same time, however, the classical, more naturalistic style continued. It is seen in the slightly earlier New Testament panels at S. Apollinare Nuovo, contrasting with the stylized elegance of the processions below them. Here a love of drama and vivid narrative dominates, just as it had dominated for centuries in Roman art (*Ill. 59*).

It was during these years (fourth–sixth century AD) that the iconography of the Christian story which is so familiar to us all was first evolved. We must now look briefly at some of the most important works that have survived, at Rome, Constantinople and elsewhere.

59 Mosaic from the upper register of the walls of S. Apollinare Nuovo at Ravenna, *c.* 520; the separation of the sheep and goats. The squat, dumpy figures and rather clumsy poses contrast markedly with the tall, elegant figures and repeated rhythm of the processions of saints in the lower register (*Ill. 56*) ▶

58 Above: Mosaic panel from San Vitale, Ravenna, depicting the empress Theodora. The frontal poses, the large staring eyes and the colourful treatment of dress and jewellery attest the heritage of the oriental tradition in Byzantine art

They will nearly all be in mosaic, for that was the medium favoured by the rich and powerful. Painting was used only by the poorer churches which could not afford mosaic.

The walls of S. Maria Maggiore at Rome boast no less than forty-two scenes from the Old Testament (*Ill. 60*) set up between 432 and 440. The colours are brilliant, the figures impressive and there is an obvious love of naturalistic settings. New Testament cycles, comprising a similar number of scenes, seem to have developed a little later. That of S. Apollinare Nuovo at Ravenna (*c.* 500) has already been mentioned. Made as it was under the patronage of Theodoric the Goth, who adhered to the Arian heresy, the selection of scenes no doubt deviated to some extent from what it would have been in a purely Orthodox church. The actual rendering, however, would have been much the same. It differs in many ways from the earlier examples in Rome. Backgrounds are reduced to a minimum, the figures are less elegant and dignified and their proportions are dumpy; yet the work is characterized by an intense sincerity which lends it great distinction. The twenty-six scenes from Christ's Life and

60 Mosaic, Sta Maria Maggiore, Rome, 432–40. There were originally 42 panels, all depicting scenes from the Old Testament, along the walls of the nave; 27 now survive. Here Jacob is shown negotiating for land

61 The dome of the Baptistry of the Orthodox, Ravenna. The interior of this building is almost entirely covered with mosaics, which date from soon after 440. At the summit of the dome is the baptism, below the 12 Apostles, and below again architectural compositions which derive ultimately from those which were so popular at Pompeii

Passion are wholly narrative in content and they tell their story expressively and clearly (*Ill. 59*).

The mosaic ceiling of the Baptistry of the Orthodox, also at Ravenna, on the other hand, is essentially symbolic; no figures are included, but the basically Christian nature of the composition is manifest and the mosaics convey a profound intensity of faith in quite a different way, for they are wholly symbolic. They depict thrones, on four of which are open books, before a formal architectural background. The books represent the teaching of the four Evangelists. The architectural backgrounds (*Ill. 61*) derive ultimately from those which were so popular at Pompeii. But at the same time the compositions are new and original, and represent one of the most effective and lovely pieces of non-figural art that we know. Even if

62 Mosaic over the door of the Mausoleum of Galla Placidia at Ravenna, *c.* 440. Christ is shown as a youthful, beardless figure, reminiscent of the classicul Apollo. The sheep symbolizing his flock form part of a beautiful naturalistic landscape

the architecture, the thrones, the Gospel books which are depicted are recognizable as such, the composition as a whole brings us back once more to the world of abstraction which we encountered in certain phases of early art. It shows once again that the presence of living forms or the depiction of actual events are not necessary corollaries of great art.

Another aspect of the debt that these Christian mosaics owe to the art of earlier times is to be found in the Mausoleum of Galla Placidia at Ravenna, where the mosaics date from *c.* 440. The lovely composition over the west door, showing Christ as the Good Shepherd (*Ill. 62*), reproduces very closely renderings of the same theme that appeared in the catacombs, notably in those of Callixtus and Priscilla. The Ravenna mosaic is, however, a work of greater quality than were any of the catacomb paintings, for it is accomplished and

63 Mosaic of Christ in the church of SS. Cosmas and Damian, Rome, 526–30. The figure stands before a composition of pinkish dawn-clouds, and the conception is wholly spiritual ▶

refined as well as sincere and expressive. Indeed, it is perhaps the most outstanding single mosaic of the fifth century that has survived, for the colours are of great beauty, the composition effective and balanced, and the whole scene redolent of an atmosphere of profound calm.

Both here and in the mosaic in the apse of S. Vitale, set soon after 520, Christ is shown beardless (*Ill. 64*); the conception of the youthful figure of Orpheus or Apollo still dominates. But in the apses of the Church of S. Pudenziana (384–9) and SS. Cosmo and Damian at Rome (526–30) Christ has a heavy black beard (*Ill. 63*). In the latter church he seems to be, as it were, suspended before a background of pale dawn-clouds, and the mosaic has the character of a supernatural vision rather than the depiction of a living figure. Here emphasis is laid on a conception which is not only in closer accord with the expressive trend of Eastern art as we saw it at Dura, but also reflects the Old Testament conception of the Divine figure as one of awe. This is not Christ the Son of Man, but rather the Father Almighty, the ultimate judge. From the artistic point of view this mosaic is no less effective than that at the west end of the Mausoleum of Galla Placidia (*Ill. 62*), but the interpretation it puts upon the nature of Christ is very different. In the one there is a lightness of touch, a gentleness and a love of pure beauty which heralds the outlook of the Renaissance; in the other the figure is grand and impressive, heralding the large portraits of Christ the Almighty which were later to dominate every Byzantine church from the summit of the central dome, a God of Judgement rather than compassion. One might compare the former to a Renoir, the latter to a Rouault; both are great works of art, but their basic character is wholly distinct.

Mosaics that were closely similar to those in Rome and Ravenna were also being set up at much the same time in the East Christian world. The best of them were technically even more competent and perhaps even more masterly in design than those in the West, if the decoration of the rotunda known as the Church of St George at Salonica can be taken as a guide. This building had once been the mausoleum of the Roman Emperor Galerius; it was converted into a Christian church and decorated with mosaics probably at the end of the fourth or early in the fifth century. Some of the mosaics are

64 Mosaic in the apse of S. Vitale, Ravenna, *c.* 520. The youthful, beardless Christ, here shown enthroned between two angels, S. Vitale and archbishop Ecclesius, the founder of the church, may be contrasted with the much more mystical rendering in SS. Cosmas and Damian at Rome (*Ill. 63*)

purely decorative, but in the dome there was an immense architectural composition with figures of saints standing with arms raised in the pose of prayer in front of it (*Ill. 66*). The architectural backgrounds, like those in the Baptistry of the Orthodox at Ravenna, derive from the old architecture-scapes of Pompeii, but they are more realist, more impressive and the figures have an almost Attic grandeur, so that the two together produce a work of very great beauty. It is a tragedy that only a part of this great decoration survives.

A mosaic in the apse of another church at Ṣalonica which is usually known as Hosios David is probably rather later in date (*Ill. 65*). As a composition it is less effective, for it is somewhat over-full and crowded. It depicts the Vision of the Prophet Ezekiel – the Christ who was to come, before a glory supported by the four beasts which later came to symbolize the Evangelists; the man, the lion, the bull and the eagle. Small figures representing the Prophets Ezekiel and Habakkuk are at either side. Technically the mosaic is proficient and it is also very colourful; silver and gold cubes are used sparsely, but with considerable skill, to produce a lovely scintillating effect. There must once have also been another fine apse mosaic in the great basilical church of the Achieropoietos in the same town; it has, alas, perished, but small decorative panels survive below the arches of the nave arcades; the work is of exceptionally high quality and serves to indicate how delightful these decorative, non-representational, though at the same time naturalistically conceived, panels could be.

65 Detail of the mosaic in the apse of the church of Hosios David, at Salonica, of the fifth century. The mosaic depicts the Vision of Ezekiel, the Christ on an orb, with the four figures that later became the symbols of the Evangelists, supporting it. The work is accomplished, but the composition somewhat over-full

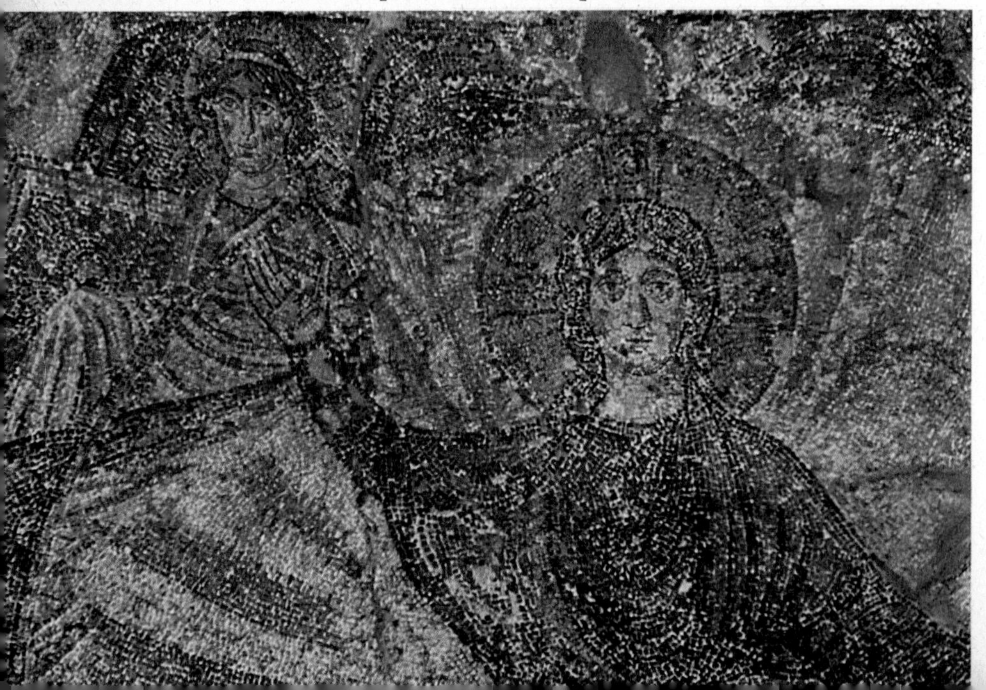

66 Portion of the great architectural composition surrounding the lower section of the dome of St George at Salonica, early fifth century. This clearly derives from the 'architecture-scapes' of Pompeii, though here figures in the *orans* (praying) position stand before the buildings, which are of a formal character

PAINTING IN BOOKS

For the last important medium of the Byzantine painter we go from one extreme to the other – from the gleaming expanses of mosaic walls and domes to the pages of illuminated manuscripts. In contrast to the art we have been discussing, the manuscripts hardly ever employ symbolism. Narrative is almost always their prime concern, usually interpreted in the most direct and literal way.

67 Illustration from a copy of Virgil in the Vatican, known as the 'Codex Romanus'. Many of the subjects illustrated occur also in the floor mosaics, for example those of the great Palace at Constantinople. The work has an almost childish naivety which is not without charm

The most complete example to have survived from this period is the Vienna Genesis (*Ill. 69*), which must have been illustrated either in the later fifth or earlier sixth century. Here the Genesis stories are told with great vividness, and the painter took an obvious delight in the rendering of picturesque backgrounds. The source of his style – or at least the main source – is ancient Roman book illumination, of which few examples now remain, but which was of course familiar to the Byzantines. We may compare this Vienna Genesis with, for instance, the Vatican Virgil (*Ill. 67*) or the Ambrosian Iliad. It is clear, however, that whatever the connexion may be, the later work shows a feeling for drama and a new command of expression that is by no means classical and which parallels the change in style already noted in other media.

This is even more marked in what is, artistically speaking, the finest manuscript of the age, the Rossano Gospels. Only a portion survives, which includes the portrait of one of the Evangelists and the illustration of a number of scenes from Our Lord's Life and Passion. The portrait of the Evangelist is interesting, for it is the first example we have of a feature that was to become well-nigh universal in Byzantine art. Later on almost every copy of the Gospels has a portrait of each of the Evangelists at the beginning of his Gospel. The scenes left a similar heritage, for the iconography was now becoming firmly established; indeed, in many of them there was to be little change until the time of the Renaissance. The Entry into Jerusalem (*Ill. 70*) and the story of the Wise and Foolish Virgins are perhaps the finest;

68 Illustration from the Sinope manuscript, sixth century; Christ healing two blind men. This is a purple codex, and there is reason to believe that these were produced under imperial patronage. This particular example, which originally comprised the four Gospels, has usually been attributed to a scriptorium working in Asia Minor

both are convincing, both decorative and the elegance of the old classical trend and the expressive manner of the Eastern have here been most subtly blended. In another copy of the Gospels, that known as the Sinope fragment in the Bibliothèque Nationale, the more dramatic Eastern elements in art are to the fore, and the figures are agitated and uneasy (*Ill. 68*).

There has been a good deal of dispute as to where the illustrations of the various manuscripts that have survived were produced; some have attributed them to Constantinople while others have sought to assign them to Asia Minor or even to Syria, where the expressive style that characterizes many of the miniatures is believed to have been predominant. The city of Antioch was of course an important cultural centre, and many of the towns of Asia Minor, such as Ephesus, were important also. But there is good reason to attribute the Rossano Gospels, and probably also the Vienna Genesis, to Constantinople, both on grounds of the style of their illuminations and also because the production of such books was a slow and

69 Illustration from the Vienna Genesis, depicting Eliezer and Rebecca's parents; fifth century. Several painters worked on this manuscript; all were competent artists with a good grasp of narrative, but this one had a special feeling for animals

70 The Entry into Jerusalem from the Rossano Gospels, very probably done at Constantinople in the early sixth century. This is perhaps the finest of all the Early Christian manuscripts that have come down to us, being in a more refined, more polished style than the others. The iconography of many of the scenes was to see little change till the days of Giotto

expensive matter and it was at the capital that the most generous patronage was centred. But it must not be forgotten that the cities of the East, Antioch and Alexandria foremost amongst them, remained important centres of Christian art and culture till they were overrun by Islam just before the middle of the seventh century. A rich series of mosaic floors covering the whole period from the second to the sixth century has been excavated at Antioch and a great many fine works of art have been attributed at one time or another to Alexandria. Nor were these great cities the only centres of culture; Syria is famed for its architecture and at least one important manuscript, the Rabbula Gospels, was produced there; it is dated to 586 and was illuminated at Zagba close to the Euphrates. A great deal of painting was also done in the monasteries of Egypt; the most important examples that survive are the wall paintings at Bawit and Saqqara, in the style we know as Coptic. They are somewhat crude in contrast with Byzantine work, but are interesting none the less.

CHAPTER FIVE

The dark ages

We have now followed the story of painting as far as the Age of Justinian (527–65), who restored Constantinople to its earlier glory and made some progress towards re-establishing the Empire of the West by his conquests in northern Africa, Italy and Spain. But the promise was not to be fulfilled. Justinian was the last emperor to rule in both East and West. After his death western Europe was again submerged in wave after wave of barbarian invasion, while Constantinople, clinging to her possessions in the Eastern Mediterranean, was often like a beleaguered fortress resisting the attack of migrating hordes from the north, and with the seventh century, the threat of a new foe, spurred on by religious zeal, namely Islam. For just before 650 the old Persian Empire in the East and Syria, Egypt and North Africa in the Mediterranean sphere fell before the advance of the Arabs, the first converts of the new faith.

Gaul and Germany passed under the control of various groups of Franks; Spain became Visigothic, until the Moorish invasions of the seventh century; Britain was the kingdom of the Angles and Saxons from Scandinavia; and Italy was occupied by the Lombards, with the Pope emerging – albeit somewhat dimly – as the effective ruler of Rome and the upholder of both spiritual and secular authority.

Barbarian art before the eighth century has no place in the history of painting; the nomadic traditions of these peoples led them to the production of portable objects of metal, precious stones and enamel, rather than of the more stable art of painting. Islamic art, though important schools of painting were to develop, was never truly European. It was really only in Rome, under papal patronage, that any extensive commissions were set in hand. The most important of those that survive are the paintings in S. Maria Antiqua in the Forum

71 St Abbacyr the Physician, wall painting of the seventh century in S. Maria Antiqua, Rome. The church is now a ruin but before it was overwhelmed by a fall of earth from the Palatine hill in the eighth century its walls had been several ◀ times repainted

72 Left: the paintings of Sta Maria Antiqua are in various styles, some primitive and forceful, others elegant and refined. One of the finest of them is this head of an angel, which is so classical that it has sometimes been attributed to a painter fleeing from Alexandria at the time of the Moslem conquest around 641

73 Opposite: mosaic in the Chapel of S. Zeno, attached to the Church of S. Prassede, Rome, 817–24. A number of mosaics in Rome were set up under the patronage of the Popes between the eighth and twelfth centuries, in a style that owed a debt to Byzantium, though the work was on the whole less good. Those of S. Zeno are the finest of them ▶

which date from the seventh and eighth centuries, but mosaics were set up in the apses of several churches in Rome during the first quarter of the ninth century.

The paintings of S. Maria Antiqua are of varying dates and are executed in a variety of styles. Some of them, like one very fine head of an angel (*Ill. 72*), derive from classical prototypes and have all the elegance and beauty of the best work in the Hellenistic style; some, like an impressive panel of the Crucifixion (*Ill. 74*), are formal and severe, with figures frontally disposed, and show relationships with East Christian art as in the Zagba manuscript mentioned previously; other portions of the work again are Byzantine in style and would appear to have been done by Greek workmen from Constantinople (*Ill. 71*). These paintings serve to indicate that art in Rome at the time was eclectic and if any truly national or local style was to be developed it was still in an embryonic state, being in the main essentially derivative. Nor are any of the mosaics of the following century of great originality, or even very high quality, with the exception of those in the Chapel of S. Zeno attached to the Church of S. Prassede, where the work is not only technically competent,

but also shows great beauty of colour and a real feeling for proportion (*Ill. 73*). The figures in all the others tend to be wooden and clumsy and the proportions are inelegant. The stylization that characterizes the majority of these mosaics was due to incompetence rather than intention; here the formalism of Byzantine art has been imitated, but without skill or true understanding.

Elsewhere in Italy painting was at a very low ebb. A few important manuscripts from these centuries have come down to us, but it is often impossible to determine where they were done. The most interesting of them is the so-called Ashburnham Pentateuch, which dates from the seventh century. Its miniatures try to illustrate literally everything mentioned in the first five books of the Old Testament, with the result that the composition is painfully overcrowded and complicated. But it does show a clear, if distant, knowledge of classical prototypes and was probably made in northern Italy, though analogues with Alexandria and even Syria have also been noted.

Manuscripts produced in Visigothic Spain and Merovingian France belong to a separate class. They are characterized by the extensive use of abstract, non-representational motifs, such as were traditional in the North and in Asia but had not been seen in Mediterranean Europe for centuries. But before pursuing this subject, we must say something more about the Byzantine world, for it was to remain for a good many centuries the main centre of culture and therefore the most important home of art in the whole of Europe.

Though there was no clear break in the story of art as a whole at the end of Justinian's reign, there is something of a hiatus in the story of painting, and it is hard to say today how much this is to be attributed to the destruction of the monuments in succeeding ages and how much to a decline in production as a result of economic difficulties which set in when Justinian died. It was, we know, a somewhat impoverished age, for Justinian's enterprises had emptied the treasury and none of his more immediate successors was very competent at filling it again. But in certain fields, more especially that of silverwork, there was considerable activity and it may well be that more paintings and mosaics were produced than we know of from the records or from what survives. We can however point

74 The Crucifixion, mid-seventh century. This is one of the best preserved of the paintings in S. Maria Antiqua at Rome, and belongs to an oriental tradition, where Christ wears a long robe or collobium in place of the loincloth usual in the Byzantine world

77 Opposite: mosaic in the conch of the apse of the church in the monastery of St Catherine, Mount Sinai. It is to be dated *c.* 565. The scene represented is the Transfiguration, an event which reputedly took place on this very mountain ▶

75 Above: mosaic on one of the eastern piers of the basilica of St Demetrius at Salonica. This one dates from between 610 and 641 and depicts the saint between a bishop and a man who is probably to be identified as the Prefect Leontius, the first benefactor of the church

76 Right: another mosaic in the church of St Demetrius, Salonica; it shows the saint with two suppliants, children, beside him. It is probably to be dated to the eighth century

to one or two works in the East of great consequence, such as the apse mosaic, depicting the Transfiguration (*Ill. 77*), in the Monastery of St Catherine on Mount Sinai, set up while Justinian was still on the throne, and to two other fine though fragmentary mosaics both in Cyprus, one of them done towards the end of the sixth and the other in the seventh century. There are also remnants of an impressive mosaic decoration which was set up in the Church of St Demetrius at Salonica during the sixth, seventh and eighth centuries. The subject-matter of these mosaics is somewhat unusual, for instead of depicting the usual narrative composition drawn from the Bible, they consist of portraits of St Demetrius, the patron saint of the church, and in most cases there are suppliants before him. On a panel, of the seventh century, he is shown as a deacon; on another, two children are presented to him (*Ill. 76*), and on a third, perhaps the best known of the mosaics in the church, he stands between a bishop and a secular figure who probably represents the Prefect Leontius, the first benefactor of the church (*Ill. 75*). It was apparently set up when the building was restored after a fire during the reign of Heraclius (610–41). Some of the other mosaics depicting the saint may be as late as the eighth century.

These mosaics have perhaps rather more the character of individual panels than of full-scale wall decorations and they suggest a comparison with the few icons of early date that have come down to us. Until quite recently our store of such things was very meagre, the vicissitudes of time having led to grievous destruction. But within very recent years the material at our disposal has been considerably increased thanks, on the one hand, to the cleaning of panels which had been subsequently overpainted and, on the other, to the discovery in the Monastery of St Catherine on Mount Sinai of a great store of material, the existence of which had previously escaped notice. This collection combines work of all ages, from as early as the sixth to as late as the nineteenth century, some of it presumably done locally, but much representing importations from elsewhere. Some of the earlier panels may thus have been executed at Alexandria, which was no doubt an important centre of painting though we know it better as the home of an active school of ivory carving which went on producing work of quality till the city was overrun by the Moslems just before the middle of the seventh century; others were certainly imports from Constantinople. Several different styles can be distinguished. Thus a very fine portrait of St Peter (*Ill. 81*) which is grand, sophisticated and impressive, shows him in a classical costume and has many of the qualities of classical art, is perhaps to be assigned to Constantinople. A panel bearing the Virgin enthroned with the Child on her knees, with saints on either side (*Ill. 79*), is more oriental, for the figures are severe and frontal, the eyes wide and staring; but even here the two angels in the background recall classical prototypes. Both panels are to be dated to the sixth or early seventh century. The full oriental style is to be seen in a panel of slightly later date depicting the Crucifixion (*Ill. 78*), severe and expressionist in character, with the figures in the frontal pose and distinct from a Byzantine version of the subject in that Christ wears the long robe or *collobium* proper to Syrian art, just as he did in the wall painting in S. Maria Antiqua (*Ill. 74*), or in the depiction of the scene in the Rabbula Gospels. In Constantinopolitan art He wears only a loincloth. Some of these icons were executed in a form of tempera, others in the encaustic technique we first encountered in

78 Fragmentary icon of the Crucifixion preserved in the monastery of St Catherine, Mount Sinai, seventh century. The two thieves are shown behind Christ and reduced in size, with the Virgin and St John in the foreground; below the cross two men cast lots for Christ's raiment

the Egyptian mummy portraits. An interesting panel showing the Three Hebrews in the Fiery Furnace (*Ill. 80*), dating probably from the seventh century, is an example of this technique and was perhaps done in Alexandria. Once more it shows a blending of styles; the angel savours of the classical tradition, though the Hebrews stand frontally and are more oriental.

Another panel of the seventh century is preserved in the Church of S. Francesco Romana at Rome (*Ill. 82*). It depicts the Virgin and Child and is in a style rather different from that of the Sinai icons. One might almost say that here we have a prototype of the kind of painting that was developed in the twelfth century in Italy – a

79 Far left: icon of the Virgin and Child between two saints and archangels, in St Catherine's monastery, Mount Sinai; seventh century. The style is orientalizing and the icon was quite probably painted in the monastery or in some major religious centre in Syria

80, 81 Above and left: icons of the Three Hebrews in the Fiery Furnace, and St Peter in the monastery of St Catherine, Mount Sinai. Both are of the seventh century. That of St Peter, done in the encaustic technique, is in a very classical style and is perhaps to be assigned to Alexandria or even Constantinople; that of the Three Hebrews is rather more primitive and is perhaps a local work

Western Madonna painting rather than an Orthodox icon. The principal technical difference is to be seen in the modelling of the face and in the way in which the subject has been approached. Here the aim already seems to have been to make the Madonna look human; the Sinai icons embody a more spiritual approach, for the panels there were intended to be paths by which the world of the spirit could be approached. An icon produced in the East Christian world was not simply a picture, sacred because it had been revered over the centuries as a representation of Christ, the Virgin or a particular saint; rather it pertained to the spiritual world and though not in any way an idol, it was nevertheless a channel through which spiritual power could be transmitted. This profound difference between Western and Orthodox art was to become more and more marked as time went on. Byzantine art was a spiritual art, closer to the spiritual world than to this, and for that very reason a Renaissance in the sense that we employ the term to describe what happened in Italy in the fifteenth and sixteenth centuries – that is to say, the intrusion of a predominantly humanist, mundane outlook – could never have taken place in Byzantine art.

Other paintings like the S. Francesco Romana Madonna may well have been produced in Rome, but little survives. In Byzantium there was an enforced hiatus in development between about 730 and 843, for during the greater part of that period, which is known as the Iconoclast age, the Empire was controlled by rulers who held the belief that no saintly or divine personage should be depicted in art. As a result the production of figural work in the religious sphere was proscribed throughout the Empire and mosaics and paintings of earlier date were either torn down or covered over. So far as Constantinople was concerned the ban seems to have been virtually universal, and nothing from pre-Iconoclast times survives, with the exception of some decorative mosaics in Hagia Sophia. Elsewhere the ban was either not always strictly enforced or not adhered to and earlier figural works were not necessarily destroyed even if new ones were not set up. This seems to have been the case with the mosaics of St Demetrius at Salonica discussed above. In the West of course the ban was never applicable because it was never accepted; indeed, some of the decorations set up by the popes at this time, quite a number of which were done between 817 and 824, were perhaps designed to assert their opposition to any such idea, while others may have been the work of artists who fled from Constantinople because they were not willing to accept the proviso,

82 Panel painting of the Virgin in the church of S. Francesco Romana at Rome, seventh century. The painting was revealed only a few years ago beneath a number of layers of overpainting, and is one of the very few panels of these early years that has come down to us in the West

which certainly gave cause for much discussion and aroused intense opposition in the Byzantine world. One rather unusual and exceptional decoration in the Western world has been explained in this way, namely that at Castelseprio.

Castelseprio is a small chapel situated in the wooded countryside some distance from Milan which apparently served the bishops of Milan as a retreat. The building itself is simple and unassuming, but it contains the vestiges of a painted decoration of quite exceptional quality, sophisticated and in no wise provincial. It lay hidden for many years, to be discovered quite by chance during the Second World War. The paintings that survive are in the apse, and extend over three zones. The lowest is almost entirely obliterated; in the

83 Wall painting of the Nativity in the church of Castelseprio near Milan. The date of these paintings has been disputed; they must have been done before 860 and are perhaps the work of a Greek Master who felt unable to accept the ban on figural art imposed in the Byzantine world between 730 and 843

others are scenes from the early life of Christ, including the Annunciation, the Nativity (*Ill. 83*), the Journey to Bethlehem, the Presentation (*Ill. 84*) and the Proof of the Virgin, a scene not very often depicted which illustrates the text of the Book of Numbers, IV, 17ff. The date of the paintings is by no means certain, but they are definitely to be dated to before 860 because there are graffiti of that date scratched on them. Nor are the authorities agreed about the genesis of their style, but the sheer quality of the work has led to the suggestion that an artist from Constantinople may have been responsible, and the presence of certain Greek words in the inscriptions that accompany the scenes also suggests a Greek connotation. We know that contacts with the Byzantine world were established by Charlemagne – there was even talk of his marriage with the Byzantine Empress Irene – and it may well be that the paintings are the work either of a Constantinopolitan Greek who was anxious to escape the control imposed by Iconoclasm, or that of a Western painter who, spurred on by the spirit of the Carolingian revival, had learnt from a Byzantine master.

With the end of Iconoclasm in the East in 843 there dawned an age of exceptional brilliance. It is usually called that of the Macedonian Renaissance, taking its name from the dynasty that ruled the Empire between 867 and 1059. The Empire was rich and prosperous, patronage lavish and enlightened, and artists of great excellence seem to have been available to answer the call. Though a tremendous amount has perished, there are vestiges of enough large-scale monuments scattered over the wide area that the Empire comprised to give at least an idea of the glories that once existed. The details may be filled in by comparing works on a small scale, in enamel, metal or ivory, and, more especially, in miniature paintings in manuscripts, for their style was in close accord with that of the large-scale works in paint and mosaic. But before we move forward into this new age in the East, it is necessary to see what was happening in the West.

84 Wall painting at Castelseprio; the Presentation in the Temple. The paintings originally depicted a fairly full cycle of New Testament scenes, but only some of them now survive

CHAPTER SIX

Carolingian Europe

Charlemagne ('Carolus Magnus' or Charles the Great) was crowned Emperor of the West in Rome on Christmas Day 800. His achievement had been something of a miracle. He had brought together under his own rule the dissident peoples of the areas today embraced by southern Germany, most of France, Switzerland and northern Italy. More than this, his reign marked a new era for the West, a recovery of her old position as a centre of civilization and culture.

The Empire which he established was in many respects modelled on the Byzantine, but Charlemagne and his followers also looked back to the glories of Rome in search of inspiration, and the art which they sponsored was ultimately a Western rather than an East European art. In spite of barbarian inroads, art in the West had not been entirely eclipsed during the years which intervened between Rome's pre-eminence and Charlemagne's Empire. Indeed, in certain areas it had flourished with surprising brilliance.

THE FIRST BRITISH ART

Northern Britain was on the extreme verge of European civilization, yet it was here that an art of superb quality and originality arose, even before Charlemagne's unification of the Continent, capable of standing comparison with anything being produced elsewhere. Although developed principally in the service of the Christian Church, it yet owed a debt both to the pagan styles of the North and to the Mediterranean world.

That Mediterranean elements were introduced into Britain is not surprising, for the earliest Christian missionaries came from that area, and no doubt carried illustrated manuscripts of the Gospels or other parts of the Bible with them; these were copied locally, sometimes with a comparatively high degree of competence, as we see for instance in the portrait miniatures in the Codex Amiatinus.

85 Miniature from the Codex Amiatinus. It shows the scribe Ezra writing, and follows the scheme of the classical author-portrait. The miniature was done in England about 700, but the painter must have followed a Mediterranean model very closely

86 Portrait of St Matthew from the Lindisfarne Gospels, so-called after the Northumbrian island of that name where it was written at the end of the seventh century. A similar portrait marks the beginning of each of the four Gospels. They follow an east Mediterranean prototype, but the style is linear and shows little feeling for modelling or depth

87 Ornamental page from the Lindisfarne Gospels. The men who illuminated this book were far more at home in intricate, non-representational work of this type than in representational art, but they seem to have been equally good at dealing with patterns of a purely geometric type and those based on stylized animal or bird forms

The book was written at Jarrow in 716, though the most important of the miniatures may be earlier, and the portrait illustrated here (*Ill. 85*) must have been inspired by an original similar in many ways to that in the Rossano Gospels which were discussed earlier (see p. 81). But the local artists had been schooled in a very different tradition. The art that they knew was essentially non-figural, or, if it did make use of living forms, they were so stylized that they were almost unrecognizable – witness for example the creatures that display themselves on page after page of the manuscript known as the Lindisfarne Gospels (*Ills. 86–8*). At other times the ornament was based not on living models, but on stylized forms like the so-called 'trumpet scroll' (*Ill. 88*), prominent in the pre-Christian art of the La Tène phase, or again, they sometimes took on a purely geometric character (*Ill. 87*). Indeed, when the artists of the Lindisfarne Gospels set themselves to doing figural work, as in the portraits of the Evangelists which, following the Byzantine tradition, marked the commencement of each Gospel (*Ill. 86*), the results, though intriguing, were by no means as successful as were their purely decorative efforts. It is interesting to note here, that in writing the names of the Evangelists in the Lindisfarne Gospels – the Greek word for saint, *Agios*, was used and not the Latin, *Sanctus*, even though the script was Latin. This no doubt denotes some far-distant influence from the Byzantine world.

88 Right: initial from the Lindisfarne Gospels, both animal forms and stylized motifs like the so-called trumpet scrolls play a part in this decoration

89 Opposite: page from the Book of Kells, done either in Ireland or on the island of Iona, *c.* 800. Though figures are included, the style is primarily a formal, non-representational one, though in this case it is used to illustrate part of the Bible story – the moment when Satan invites Christ to climb to the roof of the Temple and cast himself down

90 Left: page from the Book of Durrow, *c.* 680. The style is much heavier and clumsier than that of the Lindisfarne Gospels, and the feeling for representation much weaker, so that the figure becomes little more than a pattern. It was probably executed in Ireland

91 Opposite: page from the Book of Kells, the Virgin and Child with angels. The figures follow a Mediterranean model at a considerable remove and are heavy and rather unattractive; on the other hand the animal interlace on the margin shows the genius of this art at its best ▶

But if the Codex Amiatinus and the Lindisfarne Gospels show some links with the Mediterranean, most of the manuscripts of this so-called Hiberno-Saxon school are almost wholly Northern in style. The Book of Durrow (*Ill. 90*), copied *c.* 680, is one of the earliest of them and was perhaps done in Ireland. The Book of Kells, one of the last, was illuminated *c.* 800, perhaps on the island of Iona (*Ills. 89,91*). Though figures occur on many of the pages, their role is an ornamental one and even an illustration which tells a story, like that of the Temptation of Christ (*Ill. 89*), where the devil tries to persuade Him to climb to the roof of the temple and cast Himself down, is a piece of decoration rather than a narrative picture.

The monasteries in which manuscripts of this style were produced were the centres of the Old Celtic Church – Lindisfarne, Iona and various houses in Ireland – but the authorities are still at variance as to which manuscripts should be assigned to which centres, except for the Lindisfarne Gospels, which were certainly written in 697 or 698 in the monastery of Lindisfarne island, a remote outpost of Benedictine culture off the coast of Northumberland.

Work which was basically akin, in that it was formal rather than representational, was also being produced on the Continent in the early seventh century, in Merovingian France and Visigothic Spain, but the Continental manifestations of the style (*Ill. 92*) were never quite as accomplished as the Hiberno-Saxon, and never left behind quite the same legacy. Moreover, the Celtic monasteries of Britain all played an active missionary role during the eighth century, for the monks travelled all over Europe and they took their own manuscripts with them. The style became popular, and a large percentage of the manuscripts that were produced in the monasteries of central Europe, in areas which today belong to France, Germany and Switzerland, owed a marked debt to Northumbria and Ireland. Indeed, the style was even adopted as far away as Bobbio and elsewhere in northern Italy.

92 The Sacramentary of Gelasius, a Continental manuscript of the eighth century. The ornament, like much of that of the Hiberno-Saxon school, is based on stylized animal forms, but on the whole they are treated with less imagination in the Continental examples than in the British. From a cross hang the letters alpha and omega, to which fantastic birds attach themselves

93 Mosaic in the Carolingian church of St Germigny-des-Prés in France, dating from the early ninth century. The subject is the Ark of the Covenant, with two angels above it; both in style and technique it owes a debt to Byzantine art

THE EMPIRE OF CHARLEMAGNE

Charlemagne established his capital at Aachen, and although he was obliged to be absent for long periods campaigning in various parts of his huge empire from eastern Germany to the Pyrenees, it was nevertheless at Aachen that both his administration and his artistic patronage were centred. Here he built his palace and chapel (the latter still survives) in conscious imitation of the Eastern Emperor, and here he gathered round him a group of scholars, churchmen, artists and administrators such as had not been seen in Europe since the days of the Roman Empire.

In painting, the style which predominated at Aachen and at the great monasteries through which Charlemagne put his cultural policy

94 Above: wall painting in the crypt of St Germain, Auxerre, the Stoning of St Stephen, 841–59. The colours are limited to reds and browns, but the figures are rendered with understanding and the story is brought vividly to life

95 Right: Christ healing the dumb man, a wall painting from Müstair in Switzerland. The Church is comparatively small, but it contains an extensive series of New Testament scenes and is the most complete decoration of the Carolingian age that has come down to us

into effect – the so-called 'Court style' – was basically representational (i.e. nearer to classical models) rather than abstract (with its 'barbaric' overtones), though in fact elements of both can be found. When important work was to be done at other places in the Empire, it was usually on the orders of some imperial patron, or a man closely associated with the Emperor, while artists who had been schooled at Aachen even seem to have been employed at quite considerable distances away. One of the few large-scale decorations of this age that survives, a mosaic depicting the Ark of the Covenant at Germigny-des-Prés near Orleans in France (*Ill. 93*), is thus to be found in a church which was set up *c.* 800 by one of Charlemagne's immediate circle. It originally formed part of a much more extensive decoration which must have been executed by artists who had been

trained in a Court school; their master might even have come from Byzantium.

There are records or meagre vestiges of quite a number of large-scale church decorations in quite a number of places. In the great Monastery of Ingelheim scenes from the New Testament were depicted on one side of the building, with the Old Testament parallel on the opposite wall, and originally there were certainly also paintings at St Gall. An extensive decoration of the same type (*Ill. 95*) survives in comparatively good condition in the much smaller Church of Müstair in Switzerland which dates from the ninth century. Paintings in the crypt of the Church of St Germain at Auxerre in France may also be noted; they show the Stoning of St Stephen (*Ill. 94*) and date from between 841 and 859.

A far better idea of the quality of Carolingian painting may however be gathered from a study of the manuscripts. Quite large numbers of these survive and nearly all are in excellent condition, for the Carolingian illuminators were not only great artists, but also very expert technicians. These manuscripts have attracted the attention of scholars over a long period, and it has proved possible, sometimes on the basis of colophons or other written evidence, and sometimes on that of style, to assign the examples to a number of different schools.

The most important of these was at Aachen, the capital, and it was at its most productive between 795 and 814. Several superb copies of the Gospels may be attributed to it, notably the so-called Gospels of Charlemagne (*Ill. 96*), now at Vienna, and another copy now at Aachen (*Ill. 97*). Both are illustrated in a grand, but more

96 Left: St Matthew, from the Gospels of Charlemagne, painted before 800 at the imperial centre of Aachen

97 Opposite: page from another Gospel manuscript produced at Aachen, showing the four Evangelists in a conventionalized landscape, each accompanied by his symbol ▶

INVIGILIA NATALIS

98 Opposite: The Fountain of Life from the Godescalc Gospels, 781. A circular building like a Greek tholos is topped by a cross and surrounded by birds and animals. Similar compositions occur in other manuscripts of the period; they represent one of the most delightful of the Carolingian contributions to art ◀

99 Right: another page from the Godescalc Gospels, 781, Christ blessing. Certain details, like the throne and the sausage-shaped cushion are common to Carolingian and Byzantine art, but the Carolingians never adopted the bearded, awesome Christ, preferring the youthful, beardless type which had dominated in Early Christian art in Italy

or less conventional style. The influences of Byzantine models is often easy to recognize, but there are also radical differences in both style and subject-matter. It is more mundane and less spiritual; portraits of Evangelists appear less frequently at the beginning of their Gospels, and far greater prominence is given to imperial scenes, with the Emperor enthroned among his courtiers.

The miniatures of the so-called Godescalc Gospels (781) are particularly attractive; they include not only a very impressive frontispiece of Christ (*Ill. 99*) but also a lovely composition depicting the

Fountain of Life (*Ill. 98*), a sort of temple with animals grouped round it. This is a unique work, both for its delight and charm (qualities which are rare enough in Carolingian art) and for the strong element of conscious 'Renaissance' which it displays: the architectural landscapes of Pompeii have returned in the pages of a devotional book! This is not the only instance of classicism in the Godescalc Gospels – the portrait of Christ, for example, shows a cleanshaven youth instead of the impressive bearded figure which had been universally accepted in the Eastern world even before Iconoclasm. In other works of the Aachen school, and especially in the decorative borders and initials, the 'Barbaric' style of the North can be seen lingering side by side with the new 'Renaissance' elements. The influence of the Hiberno-Saxon school is evident in the Gospel Book of Trier (*Ill. 100*), which shows interlacing ornament of a wholly Northern character.

Though the school of painting that was established at Aachen was no doubt the most important, several other schools were active even before 800, and most of them continued to work, even after the fall of the Carolingian dynasty – some were even still in existence in later medieval times. One, known as the 'Ada group', is really a separate sub-group of the Aachen school and about ten manuscripts are to be assigned to it. But other schools were essentially local, like that at Tours, founded by Alcuin in 796. It was responsible for the production of quite a number of manuscripts executed for imperial patrons, like the Bible of Charles the Bald (*Ill. 102*) or the Gospels of Lothair, done in 851 (*Ill. 104*), both of them books of great magnificence. The school was brought to an end by Norse invasions in 853.

The court school of Charles the Bald developed out of that at Tours and achieved prominence thanks to the presence there of a man named Liuthard; his most outstanding production was probably the Codex Aureus of St. Emmeram, now at Munich, written in 870 (*Ill. 103*). Seldom has a richer or more lavish manuscript ever been executed, for gold was used with great profusion, the colours are rich and brilliant and there is a mass of decoration. As in nearly all the Carolingian manuscripts the craftsmanship was of very high

100 The opening page of St John's Gospel, from the Gospel Book of Trier. The first word 'In' is treated with lavish decoration, then follows the rest of the sentence in more conventional lettering, 'principio erat verbum' – 'In the beginning was the word'

quality, and the miniatures are still in almost pristine condition. The school reached its apex *c.* 880.

The school of Metz was less clearly defined, but the illuminators who worked there would seem to have preferred creating elaborate initial letters rather than full-page illuminations, while at Rheims they liked vigorous monochrome drawings, if one may judge by the most important work attributed to that school, the famous Utrecht Psalter, dating from *c.* 832 (*Ills. 105–6*). Its illustrations are all in line and show the school's work at its best, for the delicate, rather nervous handling which was characteristic of Rheims is well suited to line drawing, In colour, Rheims work tended to be somewhat mannered, and the Evangelist portraits in the Gospels of Ebbo at Epernay, done between 816 and 835, are almost grotesque, so

101 An Evangelist from the Gospel Book of Ebbo, done at Rheims between 816 and 835. The nervous linear style typical of the drawing of the Rheims school (e.g. the Utrecht Psalter) was also adopted in painting, but in that medium the results were disconcerting

102 Title-page from the Bible of Charles the Bald, ninth century, showing the book itself (carried by monks on the left) being presented to the Emperor (centre) by Count Vivian of Tours (on the right)

agitated is the draughtsmanship (*Ill. 101*). This strange, jittery manner clearly had little future in paint, though the style of some of the thirteenth-century sculptures on the cathedral at Rheims is almost equally fussy. The line drawings of the Rheims school, on the other hand, were to leave an important heritage, as we shall see when we come to study the manuscripts of the later Saxon period in England.

103 Opposite: page from the Codex Aureus of St Emmeram, written in 870 by the scribe Liuthard. The colouring is especially rich, gold being used with great ◀ profusion

104 The emperor Lothair, Charlemagne's grandson, from the Gospels of Lothair done at Aachen in 851. The monumental treatment of the patron accords with a taste for portraiture observable in much Carolingian work

MATAINSAECULUMSAE
CULI· FACTAINUERITATE
ETAEQUITATE
AETERNUMTESTAMEN
TUMSUUM
SCMETTERRIBILENOMEIUS·
BUSFACIENTIBUS
LAUDATIOEIUSM
INSAECULUSAECU

105 The Utrecht Psalter, Psalm CXI (in the Authorised Version, 112), done at Rheims in 832. It contains a series of very vivid, nervous line drawings illustrating the Psalms. The architecture at the back represents the abode of the wealthy man who feareth the Lord (v. 1 and 3). In the centre a man distributes wealth (v. 9); a group of the damned are shown in a pit in the foreground (v. 10)

The Carolingian Age was comparatively short-lived, for Charlemagne's successors were not very competent and failed to hold the Empire together in the face of a series of Norse invasions around the middle of the ninth century. But soon after the middle of the tenth century centralized control was once again established by Henry the Fowler, and his son Otto I was crowned at Aachen in 956 as king, and at Rome in 962, as emperor of a newly established state which was to take its name from him as the Ottonian. This extended farther north and east than had the Carolingian Empire.

Though the actual line that Otto established hardly survived the turn of the millennium, a new historical phase had taken firm root in the West – that of a multiplicity of kingly or princely estates rather than of great empires – and from that time on, the story of painting also takes on a new turn. No longer do barbarian styles intervene to interrupt the flow of development of figural art, no longer are there long, almost irreparable breaks in the story. From then onwards the chain of development was well-nigh continuous. Artists thenceforth moved more freely from place to place, serving one patron here, another there; centres of production became progressively more numerous, and if work at one was interrupted it continued on parallel lines elsewhere; works on a large scale were not only more frequently commissioned but also more often succeeded in escaping destruction. Thus, after about the year 1000, the task of writing a brief history such as the one attempted here takes on a different character so far as the West is concerned – it becomes one of selection from a mass of material rather than one of recording virtually every example which chance has preserved for us. But in the East, as a result of the far-reaching devastations wrought by the Turkish invasions of the fourteenth and fifteenth centuries, the monuments that survive are still few and far between and so much has been lost that the problem there is rather to try to re-create the past and to find enough to do justice to what must once have existed.

106 The Utrecht Psalter, Psalm XXVI (27). In the foreground are 'The hosts that are encamped against him' (v. 2–3). The Psalmist is in the centre before a church; the hand of God sheds rays upon him (v. 1, 4 and 5). The woman and child at the side illustrate the passage '. . . when my father and my mother forsake me' (v. 10)

107 Above: wall painting in the church of S. Vincenzo, Galliano, Italy, *c.* 1007, the Prophet Jeremiah. The style of these paintings is very individual and essentially expressionist, the lines of the faces being exaggerated to produce an emotional effect

CHAPTER SEVEN

The Ottonian flowering

Charlemagne's successors tried in vain to hold his huge empire together; the forces of division were too strong. His great-grandson Charles the Fat was the last man to claim power over all the old Carolingian territories. When he was deposed in 887 Europe was split into three – roughly modern France, modern Germany and an area in between called Lotharingia. It was in the German-speaking area, where the imperial traditions were strongest, that painting maintained its highest quality. The three Ottos, who reigned from 936 to 1002, have given their name to the whole period during which Western art could be said to have come of age.

Of large-scale works only a few examples have survived, and they are in poor condition. One of them is the series of frescoes in the Church of S. Georg at Oberzell, one of three important monasteries on the small island of Reichenau on Lake Constance. The paintings are competent but rather drier in style than was usual in Carolingian times (*Ill. 108*). Another is S. Vincenzo at Galliano in Italy, done in *c.* 1007. Here there is both brilliance and originality. The figures are tall and elongated, the style imaginative rather than realistic. Galliano shows that the qualities which come out so strikingly in the manuscripts were certainly present – and no doubt with even greater force – in the frescoes (*Ill. 107*.)

To compensate for their loss, we do have an abundance of superb manuscripts. They show the same technical excellence as those of the Carolingian Age, but the nature of the art is strikingly different. The earlier style was rich, impressive, basically naturalistic and owed much to its classical heritage. The illuminations of Ottonian times, on the other hand, in spite of their brilliant colour and a profuse use of gold, have an enigmatic, visionary character, and at times

108 Opposite: wall painting at Oberzell, Reichenau, dating from around 1000; the Raising of Lazarus. The paintings are now in poor condition, though there was once a very full and complete decoration. Their rather dry and restrained style ◀ contrasts with that of the Galliano paintings

109 Above: the Massacre of the Innocents, from the Codex Egberti, of the late tenth century. Here the treatment is much more naturalistic – even violent – than is usual in Ottonian art

110 Opposite: page from the Gospel Book of Abbess Uota, 1002–25. The Crucifixion is depicted above, personifications of Life and Death below. The composition is suggestive almost of a metalwork book cover rather than a painting ▶

the paintings are so highly conventionalized that they become almost abstract. As in the Byzantine world, it is the spiritual meaning rather than the outward appearance that artists are striving to express; this is perhaps to some extent to be explained by the fact that Otto had married a Byzantine princess, Theophano, who seems to have brought Byzantine craftsmen to the West with her. But in spite of these links the Ottonian style was very distinct, and there is no mistaking an Ottonian work for a Byzantine one.

To gain some insight into the essence of the Ottonian style, let us look at a page from one of the most extreme examples – the Entry into Jerusalem from the Gospel Book of Otto III, now at Munich,

painted between 996 and 1002 (*Ill. 111*). It is wholly two-dimensional, the ground is divided into two parallel strips; on the upper one Our Lord's donkey moves forward, while the men who cast their cloaks in His path have been relegated to the lower one. The trees have become curious, emaciated pieces of conventional form, and the colouring is strange and unearthly. The pictures look like dream-like renderings of the scene. It would be hard to think of illustrations which at the same time as actually depicting a theme are so far removed from earthly reality. They succeed to quite an amazing degree in giving expression to the more mystic elements of the Christian faith.

The same mystical approach characterizes many of the other manuscripts of the age. Look, for instance, at the Gospel Book of Abbess Uota of Niedermünster, dating from 1002 to 1025. The page illustrating the Crucifixion is typical (*Ill. 110*). Nothing could be less

111 The Entry into Jerusalem, from the Gospel Book of Otto III, 996–1002. The conception here is two-dimensional, and the figures have been placed on two separate registers, with strange emaciated forms and a strong tendency towards abstraction

112 Page from the Gospel Book of Otto III, showing personifications of the four regions of the empire, Slavinia, Germania, Gallia and Rome, paying reverence to the king. Once more the picture is two-dimensional and forms a completely flat pattern, depending on rhythm and colour rather than depth

113 Left: the Marriage feast of Cana from the Gospel Book of Abbess Hitda, *c.* 1010. Christ is shown blessing the wine jars, and these again form a rhythmical pattern which is more interesting pictorially than is the group of spectators at the back

114 Opposite: Book of Pericopes of Henry II; page depicting the Ascension, which is conveyed in a very expressive manner. A somewhat unusual innovation is the rendering of heaven as a straight horizontal line across the top of the picture, rather like a balustrade, with angels leaning over it ▶

like a direct representation of a real event. For one thing, the whole page is organized as an ornamental composition. For another, purely allegorical figures of Life and Death appear at the bottom along with real people, and even Christ Himself is portrayed less as an actual person than as a concept or idea. In another important manuscript (*Ill. 112*) figures personifying the four parts of the Empire – Slavinia, Germania, Gallia and Rome – do homage to Otto III. They are formal, angular and conventionalized, and the picture makes its effect primarily through the rhythm of the composition and the gaiety of the colours. Other works in the same style and from the same scriptorium, Trier, include the Prayer Book of Otto III and the Book of Pericopes of Henry II (*Ill. 114*). We see a somewhat similar stress on rhythmical composition in the scene of the Marriage at Cana in the Gospel Book of Abbess Hitda (*Ill. 113*), done in the early years of the eleventh century, where the wine jars play just as important a part in the composition as do the living figures.

We must be careful, however, not to oversimplify. The tendency to abstraction that has just been described is certainly characteristic of Trier and of several other centres. But others were more conservative. Reichenau and Aachen seem to have carried on the earlier Carolingian tradition more faithfully. The scene of the Massacre of the Innocents from the Codex Egberti (*Ill. 109*), produced at Reichenau, for instance, shows an extremely naturalistic approach. Elsewhere, particular schools evolved their own individual manner. The Gospel Book of the Abbess Hitda, done at Cologne, is executed in a very free, sketchy version of the imperial manner. Regensburg and Hildesheim also developed distinctive styles. Regensburg can boast the Gospel Book of Uota, while Hildesheim reflects the personality of its great bishop Bernward. His Gospel Book, done there between 1011 and 1014, is of very great interest from the point of view of decorative art; its backgrounds resemble enamels and perhaps reflect the patron's interest in metalwork, for the famous bronze doors of Hildesheim were also made under his inspiration.

The final flowering of Ottonian illumination seems to have been centred at Echternach where excellent work was done around the middle of the eleventh century, the *Codex Aureus Epternacencis*, completed in 1040, being probably the most famous example (*Ill. 116*); but a fine book was executed there for Henry III (*Ill. 117*), and there are other important examples of the work of the school now preserved at Madrid and Speyer.

115 An initial 'V' from the Gero Codex, *c.* 969, probably originating from Reichenau. Gero, Bishop of Cologne, was one of the great patrons of the age ▶

IN ILLO TEMPR

116 St John the Evangelist, in an elaborate architectural setting with his eagle above him, from the *Codex Epternacencis* of about 1024. The school of Echternach is noted for the monumentality of its forms, probably reflecting the grandeur of the lost large-scale paintings

117 Another Echternach manuscript page, showing the Emperor Conrad II and Empress Gisela kneeling at the feet of Christ. Choirs of angels glorify Christ and the roundels again contain symbols of the Evangelists

THE 'WINCHESTER SCHOOL'

Outside the Ottonian Empire, the only other outstanding school of illumination that existed in the West was that flourishing in England during the Saxon period. It is somewhat misleading to call this the 'Winchester school', since by no means all the most important manuscripts were produced there. Scriptoria of equal eminence existed at Canterbury, Bury St Edmunds and several other monasteries, including some in the West Country, like Hereford. But the name has become accepted, and indeed a large proportion of the earlier works do in fact stem from Winchester. It was a period of great achievement in English art as a whole. Stone sculpture, ivory carving, metalwork and textiles all reached an outstanding level. The miniatures, however, surpassed all the rest, creating a new style which went on developing until it was cut short by the Norman Conquest, though even after that its legacy still remained important.

Among the earliest masterpieces of the Winchester school is a charter granted to the New Minster there in 966 by King Edgar. Its title-page (*Ill. 118*) shows at the top Christ before an oval glory which is upheld by four angels; the king stands below, gazing upwards, between St Peter, holding a huge key, and the Virgin. The figures are silhouetted against an open background, and the rendering is two- rather than three-dimensional, but there is a feeling for modelling both in the costumes and in the figures themselves, and the curious emaciated appearance of the personages in the Ottonian miniatures is absent. But an even more distinctive feature is to be seen in the border, which is composed of heavily modelled leaves twining on a sort of trellis-like frame. Borders of this sort were rare on the Continent but were developed as a characteristic feature in the work of the English school. They are well-nigh invariably present in the manuscripts of later Saxon times and are often of great beauty in themselves.

Another Winchester manuscript, done some fifteen years later, is the famous Benedictional of St Aethelwold, formerly at Chatsworth and now in the British Museum. There the borders are even more noteworthy. In some there are great rosettes at the corners, made up of rich leaf patterns set on geometric frames; in others a very old

118 Title-page from King Edgar's charter, done at Winchester in 966. Christ is shown within an oval of glory held by angels, as in the normal rendering of the Ascension scene. Below, however, instead of the apostles, stand King Edgar, St Peter and the Virgin

scheme is reverted to, where the figures are framed beneath arcades. But both the arches and the columns that support them are heavy and are richly ornamented, and the capitals are even more elaborate. Within these massive borders, scenes from the Bible story are depicted with great spirit and, within limits, with great realism (*Ill. 120*). At times the figures are confused with the border, as in the scene of the Maries at the Sepulchre (*Ill. 119*), where the sleeping soldiers literally form a part of it. But even so the figures themselves are very true to life, so that this is far from being an abstract art. It is rather to be described as a figural art where a passion for majestic decoration has run riot.

119 Left: the Maries at the Sepulchre, page from the Benedictional of St Aethelwold, done at Winchester soon after 989. The large rosettes at the corner are typical of the later Saxon school; the leaves themselves are naturalistically treated, but the whole conception is essentially decorative

120 Opposite, the Presentation, from the Benedictional of St Aethelwold. The figures from the various scenes are shown realistically, but they also form part of the ornamental borders so that it is often impossible to tell where figures end and borders begin ▶

Closely akin to the Benedictional of St Aethelwold are two books now preserved at Rouen, the Benedictional and the Sacramentary of Robert of Jumièges, the former (*Ill. 123*) dating from *c.* 989, the latter from just after the year 1000. The figures in the latter are less monumental and attest not so much its later date as a more marked relationship with the art of the Ottonian world. The angular movements of the Magi in the scene of the Adoration (*Ill. 124*), as well as the way in which the faces are done, are thus much less realist and more imaginative, and in the rendering of Pentecost (*Ill. 125*) a new fantasy has entered, wherein the floral motifs of the border and the figures of the Apostles receiving the gift of tongues blend together to express, in some strange way, the nature of the event, the gift of tongues descending like a flame of fire. Here glorious decoration goes hand in hand with textual interpretation.

The light, imaginative, illustrations of this manuscript – and indeed those of the other Winchester books too – may be contrasted with

121 Evangelist from the Trinity College Cambridge Gospel Book of the early eleventh century. This is probably to be assigned to the scriptorium at Canterbury, where the style was harder and less feathery than at Winchester

the much heavier, stronger style of the illustrations to the New Minster Gospels (*Ill. 122*), now in the British Museum (Add. 34890). Here the colouring is darker, the drawing more precise and less feathery, while the borders, though present, are like frames and are made up not of foliage but of medallions containing figures which look as if they were meant to depict enamels on a metal

122 The Evangelist St John in the New Minster Gospels. The border shows a blend of the characteristic floral motifs and figure medallions which look as if they are modelled on metal forms

bookbinding. The differences are indeed so marked that one must assign this book to a different workshop from that responsible for the previous manuscripts. It would even be tempting to suggest a different centre of production, were not the volume definitely associated with Winchester.

Canterbury shows the same heavy, rather solid style. The border of the opening of St Matthew's Gospel (*Ill. 126*), in a manuscript done for the Monastery of Christ Church there early in the eleventh century and now in the British Museum, is characteristic, for the frame has become detached and constitutes a distinct entity in itself, unlike those of the earlier Winchester manuscripts. The same is true of what is no doubt the finest of all the manuscripts of this group (*Ill. 121*), a copy of the Gospels at Trinity College, Cambridge (B. 10. 4). Its miniatures are grand and impressive and it is certainly to be counted as one of the finest of these Anglo-Saxon manuscripts,

123 Opposite: the Maries at the Sepulchre, from the Benedictional of Robert of Jumièges of about 980. Compare this with the slightly earlier Benedictional of ◀ St Aethelwold (*Ill. 119*)

124, 125 Below: two scenes from the Sacramentary of Robert of Jumièges, dating from *c.* 1000; Adoration of the Magi and Pentecost. Though in a lighter more feathery style than the Benedictional, this was probably also done at Winchester

even if the style is harder and the drawing less feathery than in the Benedictional of St Aethelwold.

It is clear that many other centres were capable of producing equally powerful work. One in the Bodleian Library at Oxford (Douce 296) may thus be assigned to Croyland on the basis of its calendar; it contains a striking figure of Christ (*Ill. 127*) surrounded by a border rather like a carved picture-frame. A manuscript of the Gospels at York (*Ill. 128*), with portraits of the Four Evangelists, may perhaps have been done there; here the borders are plain and the drawing is much more reticent. The Evangelist portraits in a copy of the Gospels at Hereford (*Ill. 129*) are again in a different style; they look almost like wood carvings, and it is possible that this very distinctive manner was associated with the West Country. However, as this question of association of manuscripts with different areas or scriptoria on the basis of style has been but little investigated, it is as yet possible only to hint at classifications which may one day be firmly established by such methods.

126 Page from a Gospel Book of the early eleventh century probably made at Canterbury. The rather more stylized border and the single letter it envelops show it to be the work of a less ambitious, less accomplished master than most of those who worked at Winchester and Canterbury

127 Opposite: Christ treading on the Asp and Basilisk, from a calendar probably produced at Croyland. It has a crisp linear quality that makes it extremely distinctive

SCS MARCUS

These colourful illuminations however only constitute one aspect of Anglo-Saxon book illustration. Works in line, either wholly in monochrome, or occasionally lightly tinted in another colour, were equally important, and large numbers of examples survive. They seem to have been produced even before the colourful style was evolved, for there is an impressive figure of Christ with St Dunstan at His feet (*Ill. 130*) in a copy of Ovid in the Bodleian Library at Oxford (Auct. F. IV, 32) dated *c.* 960, which used to be at Glastonbury in St Dunstan's time and according to tradition was drawn by him. A great deal of line work was also done at Canterbury. Some of it was apparently wholly original, like the figure of the Personification of Philosophy (*Ill. 131*) in a manuscript now in Trinity College at Cambridge (O. 3. 7), but other work was copied directly from the Utrecht Psalter, the important Carolingian manuscript which we have already noted as an example of the Rheims school. It was housed in the Canterbury library over a considerable

128 Opposite: portrait of the Evangelist Mark from a copy of the Gospels at York and probably made there. The borders are plain and the drawing rather more reticent than in manuscripts from the scriptoria of Winchester or Canterbury

129 Right: The Evangelist Luke from the Hereford Gospels. The work is again in a very distinctive manner, severely stylized with regard to the figure and with the ornamental border reduced to the small decorative floral designs at the corners

130, 131 St Dunstan at the feet of Christ, drawn in 960, probably at Glastonbury – it has even been attributed to St Dunstan himself. The style is a distinct one, firm, hard and determined and quite different from that of the Canterbury manuscripts like the Personification of Philosophy (right) in a manuscript now at Trinity College, Cambridge

number of years, between early times and the Reformation. The original was copied at Canterbury at the end of the tenth century, page by page, text and illustrations alike (*Ill. 132*). The resemblance of the copy to the original is very close, though the drawings of the Canterbury copy are a little lighter and more feathery than those of the original, and here and there the miniaturist has miscalculated and found that the space at his disposal was not quite large enough, so that he has had to distort some of his figures to fit them in. But he was nevertheless a master of great ability and his drawings have a charm perhaps hardly present in the Carolingian original. The same original was copied again a hundred years or so later in a manuscript known as the Eadwine Psalter (*Ill. 133*), but here the style was quite distinct, for the drawings were less true to the originals and were done in a much harder, more solid manner. If they are compared with the Saxon copy they serve to show at a glance how different the art of the post-Conquest period was from that of the Saxon.

Another important example of Canterbury work is the Caedmon manuscript now in the Bodleian Library at Oxford (Junius II). It is a large folio volume and spaces were left for the illustrations when the text was copied; sometimes they were quite small, sometimes they occupied a whole page and some of these spaces still remain blank, as the illustrator never completed the work. In some instances the pages were divided into horizontal compartments, as in the scene of the Fall of the Rebel Angels (*Ill. 134*) ,where Heaven appears

132 A page from the Canterbury Psalter illustrating Psalm XVI (17). Here the Psalmist prays to God: 'Rescue me by your sword from the wicked'; his enemies surround him 'crouching to the ground, they fix their gaze, like lions hungry for prey'. Also in the picture are those men 'whose portion in life is in this world, where with your treasures you fill their bellies'. The illustrations copy those of the Utrecht Psalter (*Ills. 105–6*) closely

above and the mouth of Hell below, with a clear division in between, but this was only done when the nature of the picture demanded it.

Similar line drawings were no doubt executed in other centres, and secular volumes were also quite often illustrated, notably the works of Prudentius and Terence. But the religious pictures are the most important, and of all of them the most delightful is perhaps one in a volume known as the New Minster *Liber Vitae* now in the British Museum (Stowe 944), where the Last Judgement is depicted (*Ill. 135*). This is shown on three registers. Heaven appears

133 Page from the Eadwine Psalter illustrating Psalm XV (16). Christ raises Adam and Eve from the dead, and the Holy women are shown at the tomb ('for thou shalt not suffer thy holy one to see corruption'). The arrangement of the scenes and

above, its door guarded by St Peter with a huge key with the saved looking rather smug in its windows; in the middle St Peter repulses the devil, while the soul who is being judged looks at him with pathetic appeal; below the wicked are cast into Hell and its door is firmly locked on them by the Angel of Judgement.

Up to now no attempts have been made to attribute these drawings to different scriptoria on the basis of style, for the manner seems to have been a very universal one; nor have the hands of individuals so far been distinguished. All that can be said is that this

figures follows the Utrecht Psalter, but the style is quite different, the line being severe and hard in comparison

delicate, linear art was something essentially English. After the decline of the Rheims school in the ninth century nothing similar was done on the Continent and even in England the style was eclipsed for a time as a result of the Norman Conquest. But it was by no means destroyed; the same feeling for line characterizes English work in the Gothic Age, and even in Norman times we see hints of this manner, as for instance in the Bayeux Tapestry. This is actually embroidered, but must have been copied from drawings.

Just as the Ottonian Age marked the end of one era and the beginning of a new one on the Continent, so the end of a distinct phase in English art is marked by the Norman Conquest of England, and the story of art after 1066 is of a character quite different from that of earlier times. But before we embark on it we must retrace our steps to the ninth century and see what was being done in the East Christian world.

134 The Fall of the Rebel Angels, from the Caedmon manuscript, done at Canterbury in the early eleventh century. The mouth of hell below swallows up the wicked while the blessed remain supported by the arc of heaven above

135 Page from the New Minster *Liber Vitae*, one of the last, but one of the most attractive, of the Winchester manuscripts. At the top St Peter guards the gate of heaven; in the centre a soul being judged looks up pathetically, inquiring if his name is in the record of the saved; below, the recording angel slams the gate of hell on the damned

136 Mosaic preserved in the apse of the Church of the Assumption at Nicaea till 1922, when the church was destroyed in the Graeco-Turkish wars. The Virgin stands holding the Christ child before her in the pose known as the Hodegetria, while glory descends on her from above

CHAPTER EIGHT

Byzantium: the second golden age

We left Byzantium soon after the end of Iconoclasm in 843. Politically, economically and artistically, this was a period of great significance for the Eastern Empire. A new dynasty, the Macedonian, had just risen to power. Prosperity was increasing, and the wealth of the Mediterranean world was flowing undiminished into the treasure-house of Constantinople. Artistically, the end of the prohibition on images seemed to stimulate not only icon painting, fresco and mosaic but all the other crafts as well. Materially the Empire was fated to suffer decline in the eleventh century, when much of her territory in Asia Minor fell to the Seljuk Turks, for the Byzantine army was signally defeated at the Battle of Manzikert in 1071. But the defeat had little effect on art, and the marked break which is noticeable in the West in the eleventh century is not apparent in Byzantium. Indeed, although there were important changes in style and attitude between the ninth and the thirteenth centuries, they were never sudden or striking, and art evolved slowly and with its own inner logic in spite of wars, turmoils and economic disasters. And though the sack of Constantinople in 1204 brought developments to a tragic halt in the capital, there was still great progress round the periphery – in the Balkans, in Russia, as far distant as Trebizond, and even in Cyprus.

With the end of Iconoclasm, a number of major projects were put in hand in Constantinople. New churches were built, others whose frescoes and mosaics had been destroyed were redecorated. This we know from the records. But all that survives (or survived until recently) are some rather fragmentary mosaics in the Church of Hagia Sophia, at Constantinople; a figure of the Virgin in Hagia Sophia at Salonica; and some superb mosaics in the Church of the Assumption at Nicaea (*Ills. 136, 137, 140*), which were destroyed in 1922 during the Graeco-Turkish Wars.

137 Two archangels Arche and Dynamis, who occupied one side of the apse vault of the Church of the Assumption at Nicaea. The mosaic was probably set up in the eighth century, but was redone just before the middle of the ninth. It is a composition of great dignity and beauty

The Constantinople mosaics comprised the figures of two archangels in the vault in front of the apse of Hagia Sophia and one of the Virgin and Child in the conch of the apse itself. Only one archangel now survives, but that is extremely fine (*Ill. 139*). The whole scheme dates from *c.* 867. The Virgin (*Ill. 138*) seemed so tender and so intimate a figure that for a long time it was assigned to a later date, but a recent study has shown that it is undoubtedly contemporary with the archangels.

The Virgin at Salonica dates from some twenty years later, and was substituted for a cross which had adorned the apse in Iconoclast times. At Nicaea the figures of four archangels on the vault in front of the apse, two on either side (*Ills. 137, 140*), were apparently redone soon after 843, though there is just a possibility that they were actually set up in the previous century during a lull in the Iconoclast opposition to figural art. If this was the case, continuity from pre-Iconoclast times was perhaps not wholly broken – otherwise it is surprising that work as fine and as technically excellent as that in

Hagia Sophia at Constantinople could have been undertaken without some experimentation. Perhaps the mosaicists had been able to keep in practice by doing secular compositions, although no such decorations survive. We know, however, that parts of the Imperial Palace were lavishly decorated during Iconoclast times. But there are certain technical differences between the work at Nicaea, where the cubes are set in what appears from a close study to be a rather haphazard manner (*Ill. 140*), whereas in Hagia Sophia at Constantinople their arrangement is more ordered and they are set in lines which accord with the underlying bone and muscular structure of the faces (*Ill. 139*). One may say, in fact, that a linear manner gradually supplanted what may be termed the pointillist one of earlier times, where the cubes of various colours were set singly, to produce an effect by colour contrasts. Like the dots of paint in an impressionist picture they produce a harmonious picture only when it is viewed from a distance.

138 Mosaic of the Virgin and Child in the apse of the cathedral of Hagia Sophia, Constantinople. The date of this mosaic was for a long time disputed, but recent technical examination has proved that like the archangel in the adjoining vault it is to be dated to about 867

139 Left: head of archangel on the vault in front of the apse of the cathedral of Hagia Sophia at Constantinople. The mosaic dates from *c.* 867. There were originally two archangels, one on each side. Only one now survives, a figure of great dignity and grandeur

140 Right: detail of one of the four archangels at Nicaea. The technique is more impressionist and less linear than that of the rather similar angel at Constantinople. The differences are perhaps primarily to be ascribed to the earlier date of the Nicaea mosaic

The mosaic decoration of Hagia Sophia at Constantinople was of a very piecemeal character, a series of independent panels being set up by different rulers at different times. In other churches decorations were usually more uniform, telling the Bible story in a series of scenes which followed a clearly established arrangement. The model seems to have been a church founded in the precincts of the Imperial Palace by the Emperor Basil I (867–86), and it was followed thereafter in almost all church decoration, whether in mosaic or paint. According to this system the roof and walls of the church were divided into a series of zones; a figure of Christ dominated the interior from the dome above, one of the Virgin from the apse; in the upper levels were scenes from Christ's Life and Passion; below were portraits of the saints, while the lives of the Virgin and of the saints most closely associated with the building could be depicted in side chapels. As time went on the system became more and more firmly established, rules were worked out and handed down, and eventually they were also probably set down in writing, though the only written version that has survived dates from the end of the fifteenth century. In any case, it would seem that from the tenth century onwards the arrangement of the decoration was remarkably consistent in churches throughout the Byzantine world, though no actual example dating from before *c.* 1000 survives.

THE ART OF THE BOOK, 843–1204

Though there have been terrible losses not only in Constantinople but also over the whole Byzantine area as a result of wars, conquests, neglect and Moslem overlordship, the very fact that the more important decorations were done in mosaics and not in paint has nevertheless helped to preserve them, so that we actually know rather more about the style of the large-scale works done in the Byzantine world than we do of those done in the West for Carolingian or Ottonian patrons. On the other hand, taken as a whole, Byzantine manuscripts have been rather less well preserved than Western ones, and though the production of illustrated books was always important in the Byzantine world, there are, in comparison, fewer examples dating from before *c.* 1000 than there are of

Carolingian or Ottonian books. Nor are they usually in anything like such a good state of preservation as the Western examples. This is of course to be attributed to a great extent to the rigours of climate, to the damage occasioned by wars and conquests and to the neglect and carelessness of ignorant monks, but it is also possible that the illuminations were not originally as technically excellent as those done in the West. There the colours have seldom flaked away; in the Byzantine world a perfectly preserved page is a rarity. Again, most of the illustrations that we know are purely religious and the impressive title-pages bearing imperial portraits or decorative compositions like the Fountain of Life in the Godescalc Gospels (*Ill. 98*), which were so popular in the Carolingian world, are striking by their absence. We know that the classics were much read and re-copied in the Byzantine world, but there are very few illustrated classical manuscripts of this age in existence; a small volume of Nicandor's *Theriaca* (*Ill. 141*) in the Bibliothèque Nationale and a copy of the Pseudo-Oppian's work on animals and hunting at Venice are virtually the only ones we have; the former contains two full-page illustrations in a very classical style; clearly the man who produced them copied some earlier model just as carefully as the scribe would have copied the text. In the latter there are numerous small-scale illustrations, vivid, gay and informative, but not very elegant.

141 Page from a secular manuscript, the *Theriaca* of Nicandor. The style is markedly classical and suggests that earlier models were frequently followed, especially in the secular sphere, by artists working soon after Iconoclasm. It is to be dated to the tenth or eleventh century

ΜΕΛΩΔΙΑ
ΟΡΟϹ
ΒΗΘΛΕΕΜ

142 Opposite above: page from the Paris Psalter, early tenth century. Here David is depicted composing one of the Psalms. The figure beside him personifies Melody, that in the foreground, the mountain

143 Opposite below: leaf from the Joshua Roll. In spite of the classical character of the figures the manuscript is also to be dated after rather than before Iconoclasm (730–843). The story of Joshua is told in a continuous frieze

144 Above: the Prayer of Isaiah from the Paris Psalter, early tenth century. The tall, dark figure is the personification of Night. These personifications represent the survival of an old classical tradition, and the pose of the figure with shawl over her head also goes back to a classical model

More ambitious and on a larger scale is a copy of the Book of Psalms (*Ills. 142, 144*) now in the Bibliothèque Nationale at Paris, usually known as the Paris Psalter (Gr. 139). This is probably to be assigned to the later ninth or early tenth century. There are fourteen illustrations, and five different hands have been distinguished as having executed them. All worked, to a greater or lesser degree, in a rather classical style, for the figures are grand and impressive, there is a love of picturesque backgrounds, conceived in three rather than two dimensions, and allegorical figures and personifications are included in accordance with the classical tradition. Even so, the attempt at rendering three dimensions was not always very successful and in spite of the majestic proportions and the general grandeur of the work, there is a curious clumsiness with regard to the arrangement of the compositions; in one case – the Repentance of David – the painter has even failed to understand the theme he was illustrating. The psalter is a work of great quality and was obviously done in a Court scriptorium, but the accomplishment of the illuminations falls short of that of contemporary mosaics, if we may judge by the archangels in Hagia Sophia or those at Nicaea.

Illustrations of a very different type adorn another book which is probably to be assigned to much the same date; it is the Joshua Roll (*Ill. 143*) in the Vatican Library (Palat. Gr. 431). It takes the form of a *rotulus*, and the text is written in columns at the bottom, while the illustrations follow one another along the top with no perceptible break, though they do depict a series of individual scenes from Joshua's life. His portrait appears again and again at regular intervals as the protagonist in each scene. Though parts of the figures, the cloaks and the more solid features of the background are tinted in blue and pinkish red, these illustrations are really to be classed as line drawings rather than paintings. The figures, especially Joshua, are very classical, and though the roll is to be dated to post-Iconoclast times, it must have followed an earlier original very closely. What that original looked like is hard to say – probably it resembled the drawings on Greek vases of the White Ground type.

More truly Mid-Byzantine in style is another book which is also in the Bibliothèque Nationale, the Homilies of Gregory of Nazianzus

145 Page from the Bible of Leo the Patrician, tenth century. Such manuscripts with full-page illustrations must have been very expensive; they were executed ◀ only under the patronage of the emperors or the most important nobles

146 Page from the Homilies of Gregory Nazianzus, a large and lavishly illustrated book executed under the patronage of the emperor Basil I between 880 and 883. Its miniatures are by a diversity of hands in several different styles. Here we see the Raising of Lazarus, and the Entry into Jerusalem (below)

147 The Vision of Ezekiel, another page from the Gregory Nazianzus, but clearly by a different hand from that shown opposite. The style is conservative and classical, the leaf with the New Testament scenes being more expressive but much less elegant

(*Ills. 146, 147*), which was produced under the patronage of Basil I between 880 and 883 (Gr. 510). It contains a considerable number of illustrations and several hands must have worked on it. The style of one of them was not far removed from that of the best of the men who worked on the Paris Psalter, as the scene of the Vision of Ezekiel (*Ill. 147*) shows, but others followed a more truly Byzantine manner, close to that of the mosaics and wall paintings. Indeed, the way in which the scenes are disposed in registers on some of the pages is closely akin to that in which they are arranged on the walls of churches. But the colours have a greater brilliance than those on the walls can ever have had, while the figures are more dynamic, and less monumental. This copy of the Homilies is a volume of quite exceptional quality and beauty; once there must have been many more books like it, as is proved by the existence of one or two other volumes of the same richness, such as a Bible in the Vatican Library (Reg. Gr. 1) done for a man called 'Leo the Patrician' in the second quarter of the tenth century (*Ill. 145*), or the superb frontispiece to the Psalter of Basil II (976–1025), now at

148 Six scenes from the life of David; his anointing, his struggle with a bear which is attacking his flock, his struggle with a lion, his fight with Goliath, his meeting with Saul and his Penitence. This and the page shown opposite form the only illustration to the Psalter of Basil II

149 Frontispiece of the Psalter of Basil II, early eleventh century, one of the most magnificent of all the Byzantine illuminations that have come down to us. It depicts the emperor, who conquered the Bulgars, in military costume, with a group of the vanquished in supplication before him

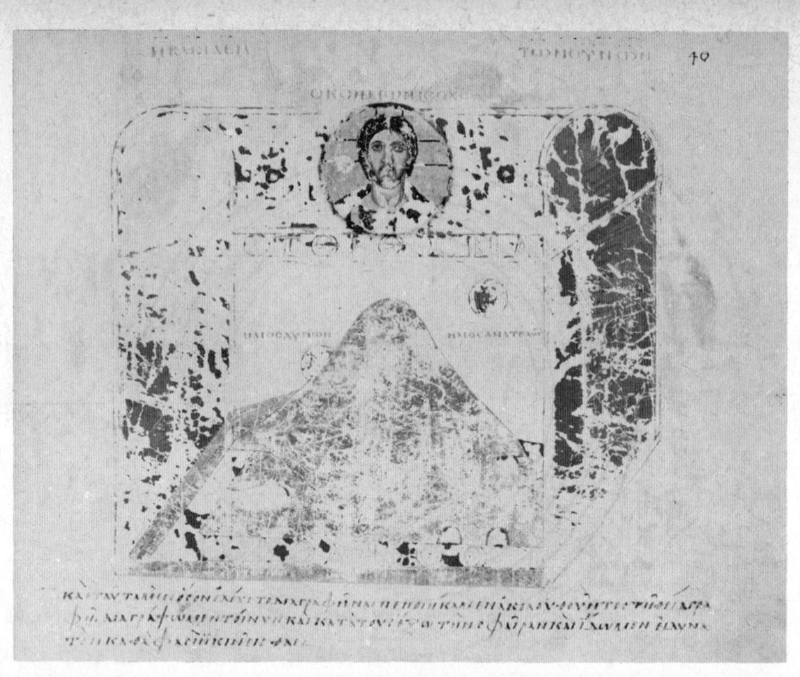

150 Page from a ninth-century copy of the sixth-century book called the Cosmography of Cosmas Indicopleustes. Cosmas made a journey to India, but his book is really a study of the nature of the universe and most of the illustrations are devoted to his conception of it

Venice, bearing a portrait of the Emperor (*Ill. 149*). Its only other illustration shows scenes from the life of David in six square compartments, all on the same page (*Ill. 148*).

One of the most curious and intriguing books of the period is a ninth-century copy now in the Vatican Library (Gr. 699) of a work first written in the sixth century, called the Cosmography of Cosmas Indicopleustes (*Ill. 150*). The author travelled to India, and the book has something to say of his journey, but most of the text and the illustrations are taken up with describing his interpretation of the universe – the disposition of the sky above and the earth beneath and of the division between the heavenly and the mundane spheres. It is tempting to suggest that the conception of church decoration as worked out for the Emperor Basil I owed something to the illustrations of the Cosmography, for the earth is conceived as a sort of box, with God looking down from its arched lid, just as a depiction of Christ looks down on the church from its dome.

However, not all the manuscript illustrations were in this grand colourful manner. Often, and especially in the psalters, they were restricted to the margins, taking the form of rapid line drawings, referring to adjacent parts of the text. Sometimes they are almost topical in character, as when the wicked are made to take on the character of Iconoclasts (*Ill. 151*). Marginal illustrations of this sort went on till quite late times; there is an especially interesting Psalter in the British Museum done in 1066 (Add. 19352) with vivid scenes showing David composing the Psalms or guarding his flocks (*Ill. 152*). Often these marginal illustrations are particularly valuable as keys to the nature of everyday life, for they depict such things as the tasks of the field, weavers at work, the erection of statues or the setting up of columns. These vivid illustrations are perhaps not always to be counted as very great art, but they are gay and lively and they make these psalters not only things of charm and delight, but also of great value to the social historian.

151, 152 In contrast to the manuscripts with grand full-page illustrations were those where small vivid paintings or drawings occupied only the margins. These drawings often interpreted the text in the light of current events or depicted themes from everyday life. On the left the Iconoclasts whitewashing an image are equated with the murderers of Christ. On the right David is anointed

153 Above: the most important churches were decorated with mosaics, divine figures being shown in the domes and vaults, while saints served as intermediaries between the spiritual and the earthly on the walls below. Here at Hosios Lukas in Greece, the Virgin and Child occupy the conch of the apse and the Pentecost scene the dome in front of it

THE HOUSE OF GOD

But it is the large-scale mosaic decorations that constitute the true glory of this phase of Byzantine art. One of the most complete of them is that in the Monastery Church of Hosios Lukas, not far from Delphi, in Greece. The monastery was founded by the Emperor Romanos II (982–98), but the mosaics were probably not set in the church until after 1000. Originally the interior of the church was very lavishly decorated with marble revetments below and mosaics above. In the dome was a figure of Christ, in the apse one of the Virgin, and on the roof of the apse the scene of Pentecost (*Ill. 153*). The mosaic of Christ has fallen, but the Virgin and the Pentecost scene survive, the latter an impressive and very beautiful composition. In the four squinches on which the dome is set were four of the principal scenes from Christ's life, the Annunciation, the Nativity (*Ill. 155*), the Presentation and the Baptism. This was a very usual disposition, although the choice of scenes was not always exactly the same – for example at Daphni the Transfiguration takes

154, 155 Opposite: two mosaics at Hosios Lukas, early eleventh century. The Crucifixion is depicted, together with other scenes from the Passion cycle, in the exo-narthex at the west end of the church; the Nativity occupies one of the squinches at the base of the dome. Beneath it the walls are covered with a rich incrustation of marble

▶

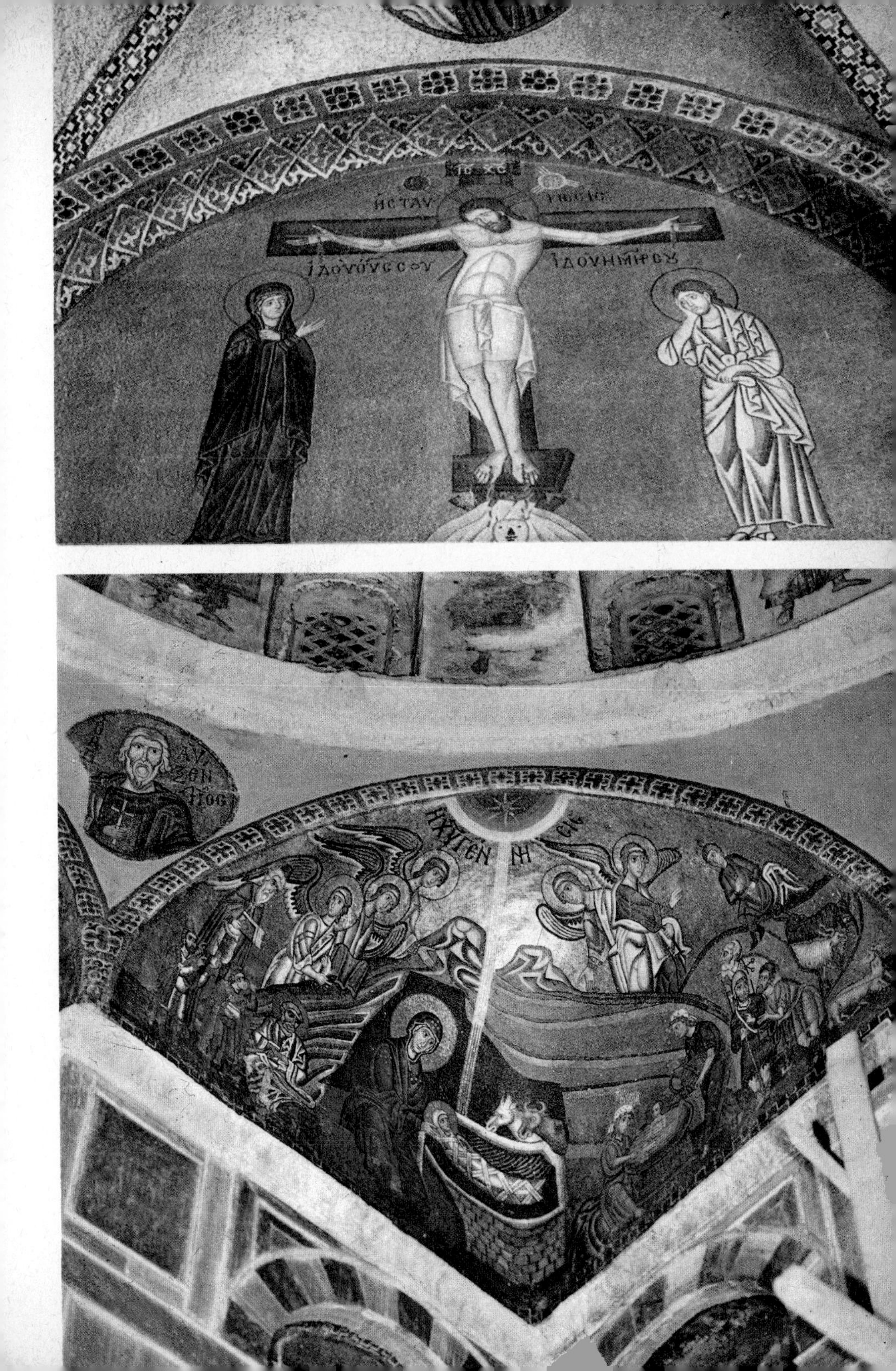
ΙΔΟΥ Ο ΥΣ ΣΟΥ
ΙΔΟΥ Η ΜΗΡ ΣΟΥ

the place of the Baptism – or sometimes the Four Evangelists occupied the four supports of the dome, as was the case at Nicaea (*Ill. 156*), where the mosaics of these subjects date from *c.* 1065.

Within the Church of Hosios Lukas itself there were, in addition to the main mosaics, numerous medallions bearing busts of saints and prophets, or even full-length figures. Scenes from Our Lord's Passion are shown in the narthex at the west end which was a usual addition to every more important Byzantine church. In that at Hosios Lukas were depicted the Washing of the Feet, the Crucifixion (*Ill. 154*), Doubting Thomas and the Anastasis – the scene where Christ breaks down the Gates of Purgatory and raises Adam and Eve from their graves, which was the usual way of illustrating the Resurrection in Byzantine art. All of these compositions are in a rather different style from that of the mosaics within the church and they are to be assigned to a separate master, for they are more forceful, more expressive – one might even say cruder – and the colours are rather more sombre. This is especially obvious in the Crucifixion, where the artist seems to have set out to express Christ's agony and the profound tragedy of the scene. In many other works the figures are more static, less emotional, and serve as symbols, whereas here the artist has had recourse almost to ugliness to bring home his message. In this respect the rendering may be compared to Grünewald's Isenheim altarpiece where similar exaggerations were resorted to with the same object.

Something of the same expressive, exaggerated manner characterizes the mosaics in the Church of the Nea Moni on the island of Chios. There the dome is set on eight squinches, in which are shown the Annunciation, the Nativity, the Presentation in the Temple, the Baptism, the Transfiguration, the Crucifixion, the Deposition and the Resurrection (*Ill. 157*). There are four other scenes in the narthex, namely the Raising of Lazarus, the Entry into Jerusalem, the Ascension and Pentecost, so completing a series of what were called the Twelve Feasts, a series of the principal scenes from Our Lord's Life and Passion. By the end of the eleventh century it had become the custom to include the Twelve Feasts in every decoration that sought completion, whether on a large or on a small scale, but there

156 The four pendentives below the dome in the church of the Assumption of the Virgin at Nicaea were occupied by the four Evangelists. These mosaics, now destroyed, were set up around 1065 and are in a different style from those which adorned the apse (see *Ills. 136, 137*)

was some variety regarding the choice of some of the scenes. The Dormition (Assumption) of the Virgin was very frequently included as the last one of the series, the Deposition being omitted.

The Chios mosaics show the same search for drama and expression as those in the narthex of Hosios Lukas – witness the scene of the Resurrection, which may be contrasted with the much more restrained, delicate rendering in Kariye Camii at Constantinople, dating from the early fourteenth century, where a more elegant trend may be noted. The Chios mosaics were done between 1042 and 1056.

This expressive manner has sometimes been associated with a stream of art which flourished most actively in the monasteries, and it has been suggested that a type of art was developed by the monks, which aimed at telling the Christian story as expressively and dramatically as possible, so as to bring it home with greater force. It was distinct from the more decorative, reticent style fashionable in Court circles, where undue emotion was avoided and where the story was told with aristocratic reserve. The difference between the two styles can however hardly be explained by assigning one to the monastic world and the other to Court circles, for the mosaics at Chios and Hosios Lukas, both of which belong to the dramatic trend, were both set up under imperial patronage. But that there were two styles in Byzantine art at this period is certain, and the greater part of the only other extensive mosaic decoration of this age that survives in Greece is representative of this other trend. It is at Daphni near Athens (*Ills. 158–163*) and dates from the very end of the eleventh century.

157 Detail of the mosaic of the Anastasis in the church of the Nea Moni, Chios, 1042–56. The work was undertaken thanks to the generosity of the emperor Constantine Monomachos, but the craftsmen worked in what is usually termed the monastic manner, lacking the elegance of the art of Constantinople

158 Mosaic of the Transfiguration in one of the four squinches below the dome at Daphni. The mosaics were set just before 1100. This polished, elegant style may be contrasted with the cruder but more expressive work of the so-called monastic school at Chios (*Ill. 157*)

Here the dome is supported on four squinches in which are depicted the Annunciation (*Ill. 159*), the Nativity, the Baptism and the Transfiguration (*Ill. 158*). All four scenes are of outstanding beauty. The areas covered by them are very severely curved, so that the central portion of each is much farther from the spectator than are its extremities, while the figures at the extremities seem to confront one another across the space in between, rather than to

159 The Annunciation, in another of the squinches at Daphni, is outstandingly successful in the way that the actual area between the two figures is brought into the picture space. At the same time the elegance of the figures lends greater beauty and spirituality to the scene

face the spectator as they would on a flat wall or canvas. The artist has taken full advantage of this disposition, somehow seeming to make the open space in the middle a vital part of his picture. This is especially true of the scene of the Annunciation, where the angel seems to speak to the Virgin across the gap between them, and so to bring the open area within the picture space. The same applies to the Transfiguration, for there the figure of Christ appears to dominate the whole area and to stand out from the wall as if projected. It is not always possible to appreciate the subtlety of these compositions from a photograph, for only when the whole of the marble cornice which borders the lower margin of these scenes is included can the shape of the area that the mosaics adorn be truly appreciated.

Other scenes from Christ's life were shown on the walls at Daphni; the Crucifixion (*Ill. 161*), in the northern transept, may be noted, for the restraint of its rendering contrasts very markedly with the emotionalism of that at Hosios Lukas. Here the figures are symbols – they illustrate the event, but do not enter into its spirit. Yet there is an elegance and beauty here which contrasts markedly with the cruder approach of the mosaic at Hosios Lukas. Elegance and beauty indeed characterize most of the other scenes and figures at Daphni, like the prophets who surround the lower margin of the dome (*Ill. 160*), and there is a new interest in the picturesque, as for example in the backgrounds of the scenes of the Virgin's life which occupy the southern extremity of the exonarthex such as the Annunciation to Joachim and Anna (*Ill. 162*). Here the fountain beside which the event took place is treated for its decorative possibilities, while the architectural elements in the background have a new and fuller role to play. The poses of the figures may at times seem somewhat rigid, but they nevertheless possess something of the grandeur and elegance of truly classical art, and bear witness to a new interest in beauty for its own sake.

160 Around the base of the dome at Daphni are full-length figures of the Prophets who foretold the coming of Christ. Each holds a scroll bearing a characteristic text from his writings

161 The Crucifixion at Daphni. Though the arrangement is formal, the figure of Christ is expressive and of great beauty

Such an impression, however, is confounded for anyone who looks straight up into the dome of the church at Daphni. Here is Christ the Judge, Pantocrator, Ruler of the World, dominating the little church with stern eyes and an implacable omnipotence (*Ill. 163*). Elegance, superficial beauty, have gone; instead we see a figure of immense power, awesome, even terrifying, but tremendously impressive, the most striking of all the figures of the Almighty that have come down to us. This figure was included in almost every Byzantine church, but it is hard to believe that any more overwhelming rendering than that at Daphni was ever achieved. In churches where there was no central dome, as was the case in Sicily, the composition was transferred to the next most dominating position, namely the conch of the main apse as we see for instance at Cefalù and Monreale in Sicily; in this case the Virgin would be placed just below, on the vertical wall of the apse.

No other full-scale cycles of mosaics or wall paintings survive in the main Byzantine centres, but there are some from the periphery – Russia, Yugoslavia and Anatolia. The mosaics of Hagia Sophia at Kiev, for instance, set up between 1042 and 1046, may be counted as Byzantine works on Russian soil. They comprise figures of Christ,

162 Mosaic in the exo-narthex at Daphni – the Annunciation to Anna. A new touch of the picturesque appears here in the charming scene of the tree with a bird's nest in it and the fountain below. The figures too seem more human than those in the body of the church

163 The great Pantocrator in the dome at Daphni. This strange, awesome figure is one of the most moving creations of all mid-Byzantine art. A bust of Christ dominated every Byzantine church, but this particular rendering remains unique

the Virgin and various saints, while the Gospel scenes, slightly later in date, were done in paint. There is also an important contemporary painted decoration in the Church of Hagia Sophia at Ochrid (*Ill. 164*) which dates from *c.* 1050, and comprises a number of scenes from the Old Testament. The fullest series of paintings of this age however are to be found in the rock-cut monastic chapels of Cappadocia, where

164 Detail of Christ from a wall painting of the Dormition of the Virgin in the church of Hagia Sophia at Ochrid in Macedonia, shortly before 1050. Here Christ's face is compassionate and tender in contrast with the awesome rendering at Daphni (*Ill. 163*)

large numbers of interesting, if at times rather crude paintings have been preserved. These play an important role in the general story of Byzantine art, but fall outside the scope of this book, for Cappadocia is in Asia. But they represent the prolongation of the style we traced in Syria in earlier times, as exemplified in the Rabbula Gospels of 586.

It is time now to look at some of the smaller-scale work, and for this we can again return to the capital. At Hagia Sophia are several mosaic panels that represent the most accomplished Court art, situated as they are in the principal cathedral and depicting in most cases imperial figures. The earliest of them, in the lunette over the western entrance, shows the Emperor Leo the Wise (886–912) at the feet of Christ (*Ills. 165, 167*); it is especially interesting for the cubes have been very skilfully set at an angle to create the best impression when the picture is viewed from below. The next panel, over the south door, is to be dated to *c.* 990, and shows Justinian and Constantine respectively presenting models of the church and city to the Virgin (*Ills. 166, 169*); the rendering of her figure is grand and accomplished, while the imperial portraits are impressive.

165 Above: mosaic over the west door of Hagia Sophia, Constantinople, set up in the reign of Leo VI, 886–912. The emperor is shown prostrate at Christ's feet; above are medallions of the Virgin, as protectress of Constantinople, and an archangel, guardian of the church

166 Below: mosaic over the South door of Hagia Sophia, Constantinople, probably dating from the reign of Basil II, 986 and 994. It represents the emperors Justinian and Constantine presenting models of the city and the church to the Virgin

167 Detail of the mosaic over the west door of Hagia Sophia at Constantinople; the emperor Leo. The cubes of the background are set at an angle in parallel lines, so that the best effect is obtained when the mosaic is viewed from the ground

168 Right: mosaic of the emperor Constantine Monomachos, and the empress Zoe on either side of Christ on the eastern wall of the south gallery of Hagia Sophia at Constantinople, 1042–55. It is probable that the head of Monomachos is a replacement for that of Zoe's first husband, the emperor Romanus III

169 Opposite: detail of *Ill. 166*, the emperor Constantine presenting a model of the city. The elaborate linear stylization of the mosaic cubes in the face is characteristic of the period ▶

170 Mosaic in the south gallery of Hagia Sophia, Constantinople, representing the Emperor John II and his empress Irene, dating from 1118. The portraits are impressive, but the style is rather severe and formal

The next panel depicts the Empress Zoe and her consort, Constantine Monomachos (1042–55), on either side of Christ (*Ill. 168*), and the last the Emperor John II (1118–43) and his empress with the Virgin between them (*Ill. 170*). They show us Mid-Byzantine art in a different vein from that of the Bible scenes, the subjects being more personal, the style more straightforward. The portraits of Constantine Monomachos and Zoe are colourful and clearly represent quite penetrating studies; those of John and Irene are rather hard and linear, but next to them is a much more expressive rendering of their son Alexios Comnenos, which was added in 1122.

OUTSIDE THE EMPIRE

Artists from Constantinople must have gone to every corner of the Mediterranean world, though it was only in areas that had commercial or political links with the Empire that real Byzantine traditions can be said to have established themselves. Some of the most important work of the twelfth century was done for Norman patrons in Sicily or for Venetians either at Venice itself or in the neighbourhood.

In Venice local workmen very rapidly learnt the art of mosaic and it is by no means easy to say which of the earlier works in S. Marco were done by Greeks and which by Italians. The later ones were entirely the work of the Italians and though the style changed in accordance with developments that were taking place in Italy, the building is wholly Byzantine; indeed the interior of S. Marco presents a more convincing idea of what a Byzantine interior was like than does that of any other church. There the decoration is complete and gives a wonderful impression of richness, whereas elsewhere only fragments remain. In Sicily, on the other hand, the buildings that the mosaics adorn are mostly of Western type, lacking a central dome, so that the effect is less Byzantine, even if in many cases the mosaics were almost entirely the work of Greek masters.

171 Mosaic in the church of the Martorana at Palermo; the Nativity. These mosaics were executed by Byzantine craftsmen loaned from Constantinople to help the Norman kings of Sicily. The church was founded by the High Admiral George of Antioch between 1143 and 1151

Of the Sicilian decorations the earliest is that at Cefalù, which was set up *c.* 1145. There is a fine Pantocrator in the conch, a figure of the Virgin between archangels below, two rows of prophets on the walls of the apse and a very decorative composition on the vault above. The work is highly accomplished and probably the best in Sicily. The same masters may also have worked in the Palatine Chapel at Palermo, where the Byzantine effect is more complete in that the eastern section of the church takes the form of a domed cruciform building. The long nave is however a Western feature

172 Detail of a mosaic in the cathedral of Monreale, Sicily, dating from the last quarter of the twelfth century; Esau hunting. The style is rather hard and unsympathetic, like all the work at Monreale, but it is also very alive and shows a real feeling for narrative action

173 Mosaic in the gallery of Hagia Sophia, Constantinople; detail of Christ from the Deesis panel (see next page). The glass cubes here are extraordinarily small, producing an effect very close to painting

and its mosaics, devoted partly to the Old Testament and partly to scenes from the life of St Paul, were done by Sicilian craftsmen taught by Greeks. Their work is somewhat coarse and clumsy in comparison with that of their masters. Better in quality is that in the little church known as the Martorana (*Ill. 171*), where there is in the narthex an interesting panel showing the donor, the Admiral George of Antioch, at the feet of the Virgin, while, as a companion piece to it, Christ is shown crowning Roger II king of Sicily. The mosaics there date from between 1143 and 1151.

The work at Monreale, where Greek masters were once again employed to direct the scheme though much of the detail was done by Sicilians, is greater in extent than at any other place and is tremendously impressive as a mass; it is not always very refined, but is, none the less, vigorous and represents an important phase of later Byzantine art (*Ill. 172*). It is interesting to note that all these great works were done for the Norman rulers of Sicily, cousins of those who had conquered Britain about a century previously.

The dynamic approach which characterizes the work at Monreale is to be noted also in a number of provincial wall paintings from Russia to Cyprus. Most important are paintings of the last decade of the twelfth century at Kurbinovo (*Ill. 200*) and Kastoria in Macedonia. But the initiative towards this more dynamic manner that we see in these provincial works probably came from Constantinople and the wall paintings done at Nerezi in Macedonia in 1164 for a member of the Byzantine ruling family serve, in the absence of work in Constantinople, to give an idea of what the progressive metropolitan style was like (*Ills. 196, 197, 199*). A new interest in life was making itself felt, and had the Latins not conquered Con-

174 The Deesis panel, Hagia Sophia, Constantinople. Christ is shown between the Virgin and St John the Baptist, who intercede with him for the sins of the

stantinople in 1204 there is reason to believe that work of great consequence would have been produced in this 'Revival' style. As it is we can assign to it two of the greatest works of art ever produced in the Byzantine world, the icon known as *Our Lady of Vladimir* (*Ill. 198*), which was painted in Constantinople for a Russian patron between 1125 and 1130, and the mosaic in Hagia Sophia known as the Deesis panel (*Ills. 173, 174*), which is probably to be ascribed to the twelfth rather than to the thirteenth century, as some authorities have suggested. The panel is of great size, but the cubes are very small and are set with quite astonishing skill. The detailed nature of the work, in spite of the large size of the panel, is indeed rather closer to that of miniature painting than to the monumental work. But the colour is subtle and harmonious and the mosaic is of outstanding beauty – the finest, many would say, of any that has come down to us from the Byzantine world.

World. In spite of its monumental size, the total effect is one of extreme delicacy. It is probably to be dated to the second quarter of the twelfth century

EGO PRI
SVM M:ET
ALFA NOVI
ETO SIMS

CHAPTER NINE

The Western inheritance

Soon after the middle of the eleventh century, in 1066 to be precise, Bishop Desiderius of Monte Cassino embarked on an extensive enlargement and rebuilding of his monastery – the mother-house of the Benedictine Order – which was to have repercussions all over the West. We know from the recollection of his friend Leo of Ostia that he invited Byzantine artists to contribute to the decoration. Although doubtless the process of Byzantine infiltration into Western art was continuous and widespread, the example of Monte Cassino was bound to be of crucial importance, since it would be followed by all the largest and most progressive monastic centres. We may, then, take 1066 as a convenient milestone in the history of painting. Until now nearly all large-scale work had been sponsored by princely or imperial patrons; from now on, the emphasis was to be on the Church, on the great religious leaders, abbots and bishops. The art which now comes into existence deserves, and has received, a distinctive name: Romanesque.

Romanesque, basically a fusion of two styles – the Byzantine and the Ottonian – rapidly developed as a new and distinct style, wholly fresh and original. It is only in a few, mostly early, examples that one can separate the Eastern and Western elements. Look for instance at the frescoes of S. Angelo in Formis, near Naples, where an almost complete cycle of paintings has recently come to light (*Ill. 175*), or the scenes from the life of St Clement in the Church of S. Clemente in Rome (*Ill. 176*), painted *c.* 1100. The rigid formality and frontal poses of the figures recall Byzantium, but the 'modern' features of the costume, the emphasis on the story and the attention to descriptive detail belong to the West. Byzantine influence, indeed, continues to be a variable quality. Such works as the twelfth-century paintings at Ferentillo, north of Rome, seem to go straight back to Carolingian

175 Painting in the apse of the church of S. Angelo in Formis, Capua, near Naples, *c.* 1060. Abbot Desiderius of Montecassino was responsible for bringing artists from Byzantium and these are presumed to have influenced the work at ◀ Capua, though the style of the work is fundamentally Romanesque

176 Wall painting in the church of S. Clemente, Rome, *c.* 1100; a scene from the life of St Clement. This is a characteristic example of the style that developed in Italy in the twelfth century, clearly distinct from the Byzantine

prototypes: compare the scene of Adam naming the animals (*Ill. 177*) with the Fountain of Life from the Godescalc Gospels (*Ill. 98*).

THE ROMANESQUE OF FRANCE

French Romanesque painting is in many ways a new discovery. Its existence of course had long been noted by historians and archaeologists, but only in the last twenty-five years have people begun to see it as something to be *enjoyed*. Now there are numbers of serious studies; illustrated books have made it accessible to the general public; and facsimiles of nearly all the more important paintings have been made and these are exhibited together today in a series of exceptionally well-installed galleries in the Palais-de-Chaillot at Paris. It is a model of what a museum of its kind should be and a real delight to any lover of the art of painting.

France is dazzlingly rich in Romanesque art. Too rich, in fact, for easy assessment. Not only were there numerous local schools, but also the individual painters were able to express themselves and to follow the dictates of their own idiosyncrasies much more freely in the twelfth century in France than ever they could in the Byzantine world. Classification is thus a very complicated problem, but in broad outline three basic groups may be distinguished. Firstly, the Benedictine, where rather sombre colour prevails and where Byzantine influence is comparatively prominent; secondly, what may be termed the French Romanesque proper, where the colours are gayer and more brilliant and where the style is close to that of sculptures like those of Moissac or Autun; and thirdly, the local styles, where there is considerable variation from region to region and where the paintings are on the whole more primitive and crude, though they are none the less often very effective.

The most impressive paintings in the first of these categories are those at Berzé-la-Ville (*Ill. 179*), a small chapel not far from Cluny, the greatest of all Benedictine houses. Berzé-la-Ville was directly dependent on Cluny, and it is very probable that the paintings there

177 Wall painting at Ferentillo, near Rome, of the twelfth century; Adam naming the animals. The style is vivid and lively, quite distinct from the heavier, gloomier manner of the Benedictine school, and possibly goes back to some of the illuminations of the Carolingian age

were done by the same masters who worked at Cluny, so that on a small scale it gives an idea of the decoration of the great church itself, destroyed, alas, during the French Revolution. The paintings must date from the early twelfth century. As is usual in the work of this group, the backgrounds are blue, the costumes richly bejewelled and the general effect is extremely majestic. A figure of Christ before an oval glory occupies the conch of the apse (*Ill. 181*), and it compares with Byzantine work in the profound spirituality of the rendering. It is a theme which was repeated with variations in a great many churches and chapels throughout France.

Even more impressive are the paintings of Le Puy, which are again to be counted as belonging to the Benedictine group. They include a Transfiguration of very Byzantine character in the porch, dating from the end of the twelfth century, and some very remarkable single figures. One of the Archangel Michael (*Ill. 180*), is little less than sixteen feet high, and has something of the awesome character of the Christ at Daphni. Perhaps the most extreme example of this more sombre style however is furnished by the paintings at Rocamadour (*Ill. 178*), which, if less impressive than those at Le Puy or less accomplished than those at Berzé-la-Ville, are possessed of a profound air of mystery, admirably suited to the atmosphere of the votive chapels they decorate.

178 Wall painting at Rocamadour – the Annunciation and the Visitation. These paintings are less accomplished than those of Berzé-la-Ville, but they are profoundly sincere and wholly spiritual in character

179 Opposite: wall painting at Berzé-la-Ville; the Martyrdom of St Lawrence. As in all the work at Berzé-la-Ville, there is great dignity and great drama

180 Some of the most striking Romanesque paintings in France are those at Le Puy, among which this enormous painting of the Archangel Michael, almost 16 feet high, is outstanding. The style is rigid and severe, impressive rather than attractive

181 Opposite: Christ in Glory, fresco in the apse at Berzé-la-Ville, France, *c.* 1100. This painting probably reproduces on a smaller scale the magnificent fresco that once dominated the apse of the great abbey church of Cluny

The second of our categories, French Romanesque, stands in marked contrast to this spirituality. It is to be seen at the height of its glory in the thirty scenes from the Old Testament which cover the great barrel-vault of the nave of the Cathedral of Saint-Savin. The scenes are set in four parallel rows, two on either side of the vault, and depict the major events of the Old Testament, God the Father playing a prominent role throughout. The colours are bright and fresh, pale greens, blues and reds dominating, and the figures are full of movement and life; for example, the masons who are building the Tower of Babel (*Ill. 184*) are real masons whom the artist had observed at work, and the effect is quite distinct from that of the majestic other-worldly style of the Benedictine group. It is still a sincerely religious art, but themes of everyday life play a prominent part, and we are far removed from the esoteric mystery of the paintings of the first group. The Saint-Savin ceiling is certainly one of the great artistic glories of France.

Paintings in the porch and the crypt of Saint-Savin were probably done at much the same date, that is, early in the twelfth century,

182 A crowned horseman, from the Baptistry of Poitiers. Rather similar horsemen appear in some of the contemporary sculptures of the region, and there has been some debate among scholars on the question of whom they depict – Constantine, Charlemagne and various mounted saints have all been proposed

183 The Deposition, at Le Liget on the Loire. The paint is very faded and the picture hard to see, but it is possessed of a greater delicacy and elegance than most other paintings of the period in France. There are a number of New Testament scenes, evidently the work of a master of outstanding ability

but they differ in style and serve to show the diversity and individuality of the group as a whole. This diversity becomes even more apparent if work elsewhere is compared, as for example that in the Baptistry at Poitiers (*Ill. 182*), or in a number of churches in the Valley of the Loire. Most delightful, perhaps, are the paintings at Chemille-sur-Indrois – better known perhaps as Le Liget – where a

number of New Testament scenes adorn the walls of a circular chapel (*Ill. 183*). The scene of the Deposition is especially interesting, for Nicodemus clasps the inert, weighty body of Christ round the waist and one senses in full the difficulty he experiences in moving it. A new degree of humanism has here clearly entered into the work.

Our third group, the local one, is perhaps best exemplified by the paintings in the crypt of the small village church at Tavant on the Loire (*Ill. 185*). The subjects are for the most part limited to single figures such as David with his harp and Samson struggling with the lion, but although they lack sophistication they are very expressive and attest the considerable natural ability of the artist. Nothing quite so personal or quite so good is to be found elsewhere, though numerous paintings exist in all parts of France which stand out because of their essentially individual character.

184 One of the thirty paintings of Old Testament scenes in the vault of the church of Saint-Savin. Here the building of the Tower of Babel is shown, in a vivid, realistic style quite distinct from the more transcendental approach that characterized the work of the Benedictine school

185 Painting of David playing the harp, at Tavant on the Loire. The church is small, and the paintings, which are all in the crypt, depict single figures rather than scenes. The style is primitive, but vigour and originality make up for the lack of sophistication

186 The paintings in St Gabriel's chapel at Canterbury, which must have been done soon after the middle of the twelfth century, are full and detailed, producing a somewhat crowded effect. The scene reproduced here depicts the birth and naming of St John the Baptist

BRITAIN AFTER THE CONQUEST

No other country can show such a superb series of Romanesque paintings as France, but new discoveries are even today still being made as churches are cleaned and old layers of whitewash removed. Closest in style to France, naturally, comes Norman Britain. Here the debt to continental models is often very clear, most notably in the frescoes of St Gabriel's Chapel in the Cathedral at Canterbury (*Ill. 186*), which must date from soon after the middle of the twelfth century. Other paintings of the period in the south-east of England, like those at Hardham (*Ill. 187*) and Clayton in Sussex of the late eleventh century, are also rather French in character. Most English examples are fragmentary and in poor condition, often the result of deliberate destruction in the seventeenth century. Only very occasionally has a whole series survived, though in recent years one of the most interesting has been revealed in the small Church of Kempley, in Gloucestershire (*Ill. 188*).

187 Adam and Eve, from the church at Hardham in Sussex. Apart from the work at Canterbury, Romanesque painting in England is best known to us from what remains in a few small village churches. The style of the work at Hardham is very exaggerated – expressive rather than elegant

▶

188 Paintings in the sanctuary of Kempley church in Gloucestershire, in a very sophisticated style. The church is a small one, in an out-of-the-way village, and the artist must have been summoned thither probably to execute a decoration commemorating some specially memorable occasion

By another happy chance one very remarkable painting at Canterbury has come down to us (*Ill. 189*). It is that in St Anselm's Chapel, showing St Paul on the island of Malta – the scene represented is that where he collects sticks to light a fire and is stung by a serpent. It dates from *c.* 1160 and a wall was built in front of it soon after, when the cathedral was reconstructed after a fire. This wall obscured the painting till quite recent times and thus preserved it. It is interesting because St Paul's costume is markedly Byzantine, following the conventional classical type with a long, shirt-like undergarment, the chiton, and the cloak passing over one shoulder, the hymation, which had been universal in the Byzantine world for a thousand years or more. The pose also follows that of a Byzantine model, and the figure is well-nigh identical with one in the mosaics of the

189 St Paul in St Anselm's Chapel, Canterbury. The painting shows an event in St Paul's life when he was shipwrecked on the island of Malta; picking up sticks to light a fire, he was bitten by a viper hidden amongst them. The style here is markedly Byzantine and the figure may be compared to renderings of the saint among the mosaics of the Palatine chapel at Palermo

190 Left: the Mouth of Hell closing on the damned, from the Winchester Psalter. The theme was one usual enough in Romanesque art, but it is depicted here with a unique freshness and originality and in a style which is wholly English. In complete contrast to the agonies of the damned and the devils torturing them, the angel locking the door is an especially graceful and beautiful figure

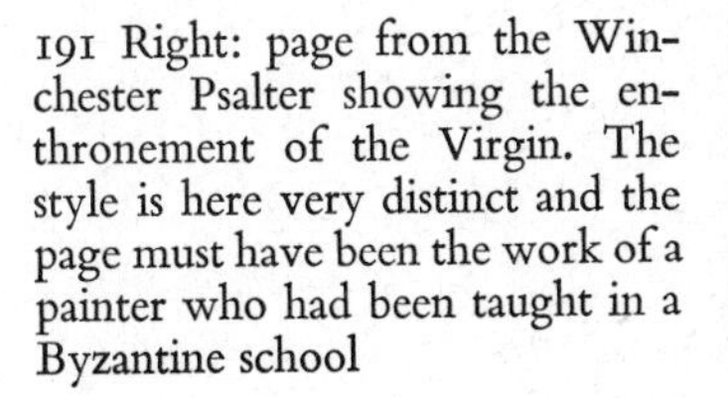

191 Right: page from the Winchester Psalter showing the enthronement of the Virgin. The style is here very distinct and the page must have been the work of a painter who had been taught in a Byzantine school

Palatine Chapel at Palermo or one in a wall painting of 1105 at Asinou in Cyprus. All these renderings may perhaps have been inspired by a manuscript model, or it may be that the Canterbury painter even saw the Byzantine mosaics in Sicily which, it must be remembered, were set up for Norman patrons, kinsmen of those who were ruling in Britain at the time; or again, contacts might have been established with Cyprus as a result of the Crusades. There were certainly very close links between Britain and the East Christian world, for some of the miniatures in manuscripts of the age are also very Byzantine in character.

The famous Winchester Psalter (*Ills. 190, 191*), for instance, was painted at about the same time as the Canterbury wall painting. Both this and the Winchester Bible (*Ill. 192*), which is still at Winchester, show Byzantine elements, but most of the illuminations done in England at this time are truly Norman—akin to those of western Europe, but with a distinct English character none the less.

Both these manuscripts were made at Winchester, but that was by no means the only active centre. Canterbury, St Albans, Croyland and Durham were some of the others. From Canterbury we have the Eadwine Psalter (*Ill. 133*), copied, like its Saxon predecessor, from the Utrecht Psalter (see pp. 117ff.) though the style is quite different and far more wide-sweeping changes have been made. The superb psalter now at Hildesheim probably came originally from St Albans. The art of illumination, in fact, which had been so prominent before the Conquest, saw a brilliant revival under Norman patronage, more especially that of Henry of Blois (1129–71), brother of King Stephen and Bishop of Winchester, for whom the great Psalter (*Ills. 190, 191*) was made. Apart from occasional Byzantine elements, the illustrations of these books show a blend of the light, feathery, Anglo-Saxon manner with a grander, more metallic style which was introduced from France. Many of them are works of very high quality and serve to attest the importance of England as a centre of artistic production at this time. Often, however, it is not always possible to distinguish the illuminations done in England from those done in France, for movement between the two areas was continuous. Indeed, what has been termed a 'Channel school' has been distinguished to embrace the products of men who might have worked either in France or in England or in both countries.

CHURCHES IN CATALONIA

Romanesque painting in France and England was not only of high quality, but also very sophisticated in character. In this it stands in contrast to that of Spain, where another very active school was flourishing (*Ills. 193–5*). Its main centre was in Catalonia, its principal activity, so far as we know, the decoration of small chapels and village churches. However, the work is all somewhat naïve and most of it is to be classed as primitive rather than as fine art. The poses are wooden and angular, the eyes large and staring, the placement severely frontal, while the subjects depicted are in the main limited to single figures rather than scenes. The figure of Christ or the Almighty before a glory supported by the symbols of the Evangelists, usually occupied the conch of the apse, the Virgin

192 An illuminated initial 'B' from the great Winchester Bible. At the top Samson fights the bear; below, the lion. Some superb book illustrations were produced in England during the second and third quarters of the twelfth century, surpassing in quality anything produced at the time on the Continent

193 Painting from the church of San Clemente de Tahull, Catalonia. Christ or the Almighty (indistinguishable from one another) is enthroned in the conch of the apse, within an oval glory, while full-length figures of saints are ranged below

enthroned appeared on the wall below, and there were full-length representations of individual saints on the other walls. Only fairly rarely were scenes depicted. It is thus a more restricted art than that of France, but in spite of these limitations the Catalonian paintings have nevertheless an element of genuine sincerity about them which makes some of the work worthy of consideration in a wider context than that of Catalonia alone. The Spanish contribution is also interesting in another respect, for it is virtually only from this region that any considerable number of twelfth-century panels have come down to us. Most of them are altar frontals, and their style and subject-matter are closely similar to those of the wall paintings. Outside Catalonia links between Spain and France were rather more obvious, as for example in some paintings in the Pantéon de los Reyes of S. Isidoro at León (*Ill. 195*), where the work is much more accomplished and the hand of a skilled master can be discerned. But the style is a good deal less characteristically Spanish than was that of the primitive painters of Catalonia.

194 The Four Riders, a page from the Commentary on the Apocalypse by Beatus, monk of Liébana, a Spanish manuscript first written in the eighth century but known to us best through copies from the tenth century onwards. They served as models both for the sculptures and the wall paintings of the Romanesque style, in Spain and France alike. The copy illustrated here dates from 1086

To sum up the achievement of Romanesque painting is not easy. One thing, however, is becoming more and more apparent: that to treat painting as of secondary importance to sculpture (as has been the normal practice) is misguided and due only to the accidents of survival. Painted decoration of the quality and on the scale of Saint-Savin can bear comparison with the sculptural masterpieces of Autun or Moissac. In painting, as in sculpture, we see the spontaneous flowering of a new spirit, a new life, which owed little to any memory of ancient Rome. Only in the next age, the Gothic, in the thirteenth century, do we see the growth of an interest in a naturalistic, figural art which was in any way comparable to that of the classical world, and even then it may be questioned whether this was due to conscious imitation of classical models rather than to a spontaneous evolution towards naturalism, along lines closely similar to those we attempted to describe earlier in this book, when the paintings on the vases of ancient Greece gradually saw a transformation from the full stylization of the early Black Figure to the full naturalism of the White Ground style.

195 Paintings on the vault of the Panteón de los Reyes, León, Spain; the Almighty in glory, supported by the four beasts of Ezekiel's vision, which later became the symbols of the Evangelists. The style is characteristic of Spanish Romanesque art, which was cruder and more forceful than that of France ▶

IOHANNES
AQVILA
MATEVSOMO
MARCVS
LEO
LU CAS
VI TULO

CHAPTER TEN

The Byzantine bloc: Yugoslavia, Bulgaria and Russia

While the great wall paintings of Romanesque France were being created, developments almost as spectacular were taking place in the Byzantine world. The first manifestations of it are to be seen as early as the second quarter of the twelfth century, in the beautiful panel known as *Our Lady of Vladimir* (*Ill. 198*), which was painted in Constantinople for a Russian patron between 1125 and 1130. The panel was then taken to Russia and has been preserved there ever since. It is characterized by a new intimacy, a new humanism, exemplified not only in the faces of the two figures, which are gentle and personal, but also by the pose, for the Child's face is pressed against that of the Virgin in affection. This denotes an approach wholly distinct from that of earlier times, where the Virgin was virtually a symbolic figure, not a mother, who held the Child with one arm and pointed to Him with the other, indicating Him as the Divine Saviour of mankind. The panel may be contrasted with the more or less contemporary but much more conservative rendering which we see in the mosaic known as the John Panel in Hagia Sophia (*Ill. 170*) which we mentioned when discussing the mosaics of the middle period of Byzantine art. In contrast to the icon, it is severe and rigid and lacking in intimacy. Clearly two trends should be distinguished in the art of the capital at this time, a conservative one which was rather hard and linear, and a more progressive one, which was intimate and personal; the Deesis mosaic in Hagia Sophia (*Ills. 173, 174*) which we described above is clearly to be assigned to the latter group. This more personal style was to exercise a very important influence on future developments both in the Byzantine world and outside it, but it is only very recently that its existence has come to be realized.

The next stage in the development of the more progressive manner is represented by wall paintings at Nerezi in Yugoslavia,

196 Detail of a wall painting of the Lamentation at Nerezi, Macedonia, dated to 1164. These paintings are noteworthy because of the humanism and intimacy of their character, quite unlike the hieratic style of contemporary Byzantine art. Thus the Virgin is shown as a woman weeping for her son, rather than as a divine figure attending the death of the Saviour of the world

197 Left: a saint at Nerezi, Macedonia, 1164. The new approach that characterizes this age in the Byzantine world is apparent in the rendering of the face, for the saint is now a kindly old man rather than an austere, semi-divine figure

198 Right: *Our Lady of Vladimir*, perhaps the most famous of all icons. It was painted in Constantinople for a Russian patron soon after 1125 and then taken to Russia; today it is preserved in the Tretyakov Gallery in Moscow. It has been considerably restored, but the two faces survive from the original work ▶

not far from Skopolje, to which we have already called attention. They were done in 1164 under the patronage of a member of the imperial Byzantine family, the Comnene, and the artist no doubt came from Constantinople, for the work is essentially metropolitan in character. The individual figures, portraits of saints (*Ill. 197*) and prophets, are personal and intimate, the scenes are shown with a new understanding of human feelings and emotions, while they were chosen not so much from the old repertory of the principal events in Our Lord's life, but rather from those where tenderness and humanism had a part to play. We thus see at Nerezi the Deposition (*Ill. 199*) and the Lamentation (*Ill. 196*) assuming a more important place than other scenes of the Passion cycle, and in both one feels that the Virgin is conceived as a mother who mourns the loss of her dear son, rather than as a figurehead of the faith. Both here and in the panel *Our Lady of Vladimir* we already have in embryo the idea of a beautiful, youthful, human mother that was eventually to dominate in Gothic and in Italian art. In the scenes of the Deposition and Lamentation we can now see the progenitors of the numerous paintings that were one day to be produced, not so much with the

199 The Deposition, at Nerezi. The choice of this scene is characteristic of the new outlook, for it expresses a more human, more intimate understanding than the scene of the Crucifixion, which had, necessarily, to be treated in a more formal manner

200 Left: the Anastasis, at Kurbinovo, Macedonia, *c.* 1191. Something of the humanism of the Nerezi paintings is to be discerned here, but the work is on the whole much more provincial in character

201 Right: saints and angels, from the Last Judgement, at Vladimir in Russia. It dates from about 1193. The figures are arranged formally, but the faces show the sympathy and tenderness which characterize the work of this phase. The paintings were probably done by a Greek from Constantinople ▶

idea of recording the Bible story as with that of moving the emotions and compassion of the individual spectator. At Nerezi we see the dawn of a type of art that was soon to attain new prominence and was eventually to reach its full expression in the High Renaissance in Italy.

But the new manner was to bear fruit in the Byzantine world before that, and during the next century a number of really outstanding decorations (*Ills. 200, 201*) were produced by artists who must have been schooled in the Byzantine metropolis in places as far apart as western Serbia and Trebizond, at the far eastern corner of the Black Sea. The earliest, and in some ways the most important, are those at Mileševo (*Ills. 202–204*) in Serbia, dating from *c.* 1235. They have been known to Byzantinists since quite early in the twentieth century but, like other work in Yugoslavia, they have not really been accorded the place they deserve in the story of art as a whole,

202 The Resurrection, at Mileševo, Serbia, 1235. The scene is here conveyed simply by the angel at the Empty Tomb, not by the Descent into Hell as was usual in Byzantine art. But there are precedents for this in Cappadocia. The sleeping soldiers in contemporary costume are particularly interesting

203 Head of the Virgin from the scene of the Annunciation, at Mileševo. The head is surprisingly realistic for a work of the first half of the thirteenth century and seems to foreshadow Sienese painting of the late fourteenth

for they are not only very fine in themselves but also show a freshness and degree of humanism which is in advance of anything of the same date known in Italy. The Deposition (*Ill. 204*) is thus expressive, pathetic and very well composed, while the Virgin in the scene of the Annunciation (*Ill. 203*) is tender and delicate and seems to foreshadow the type that was to become prevalent in Sienese art a century or so later. But perhaps the rendering of the Resurrection (*Ill. 202*) is most interesting, for it is not only fine and impressive but also presents a mass of iconographical problems. The subject, the Maries at the Empty Tomb, was not a usual one in the Byzantine world, where the theme was more often illustrated by the Descent of Christ into Limbo, but there are prototypes for it in Cappadocia and the scene follows a Byzantine convention in showing only two Maries, whereas in the West there were usually three. The arrangement of the figures, with the very striking depiction of the sleeping guards, is wholly original, while the angel is magnificent. Here the word 'Renaissance' would seem to apply better than the term 'Revival', for the whole conception of the figures savours of the

204 The Deposition, at Mileševo. The debt to Nerezi is clearly apparent – there is the same intimacy and the same tenderness as in the detail shown in *Ill. 196*

classical world, while the face is closely similar to that of the angel we noted among the wall paintings of S. Maria Antiqua at Rome (*Ill. 72*), of the seventh century. This painting is always cited as one of the most purely classical works of the Early Christian period. Another interesting feature at Mileševo are the donor portraits. These were included in all the major decorations in Yugoslavia and many of them are of real quality as portraits, apart from their great interest as historical documents.

Some thirty years later in date than the paintings at Mileševo are those at Sopoćani (*Ills. 205–7*), and though by a different hand, they clearly also belong to the same metropolitan group the style of which was quite distinct from that of any of the provincial schools that were developing all over the Balkans at the time, and which was essentially of local significance only. The work at Mileševo and Sopoćani, on the other hand, is European in its quality and importance.

205 Detail of St John, at Sopoćani, 1265. The Sopoćani paintings represent a development of the grand metropolitan type of work characteristic of Mileševo about 30 years earlier

206 Detail of the Nativity, at Sopoćani. The delicate gesture of the midwife who is washing the child, as she puts out her hand to test the temperature of the water, is particularly effective

The church at Sopoćani is comparatively large and complex; there are paintings in the body of the church, in the narthex and in six side chapels, and there were others in what was once an exonarthex to the west, which have now in greater part perished. The paintings in the church and the narthex are the most significant, the scenes being depicted with great feeling. The Nativity (*Ill. 206*), for example, is not only a very successful composition, fitting in admirably with regard to the space occupied by a window around which it is arranged, but is also good with regard to detail; the puzzled incredulity of the rather foolish old shepherd to whom the significance of the event is being explained by the younger one, or the way in which the midwife tests the temperature of the water with one hand while she prepares to wash the Child, are both things of great delight. The scenes of Christ's appearance to the two Maries in the Garden (*Ill. 207*) is interesting in another respect, for the poses of the two women were to be adopted well-nigh exactly some forty years later by Giotto in his frescoes in the Arena Chapel at Padua. But it is perhaps the majesty of the modelling and the beauty of the colouring that are the most distinctive features of the Sopoćani paintings, for the figures have a truly classical grandeur, while the contrasts of the delicate greens, the lovely blues and the subtle purples of the costumes evoke real delight in themselves alone.

207 The appearance of Christ to the two Maries in the Garden, at Sopoćani. As with all the work there the figures are tall and the composition balanced and effective. The poses of the women foreshadow some used by Giotto in his Padua frescoes

208 The boy Christ, from the scene of Christ among the Doctors, at Boiana near Sofia in Bulgaria, 1259. Though the style of these paintings is distinct, they clearly form part of the same movement that was affecting most of the major work of the thirteenth century

Another series of paintings which are of universal significance are to be found in Bulgaria in the small church at Boiana near Sofia. They date from 1259. The church they adorn is quite small and there is little of the grandeur of Sopoćani, but the paintings are nevertheless both beautiful and expressive, and the figure of the youthful Christ in the scene where He disputes with the doctors in the Temple (*Ill. 208*) is of very high quality. Once again the figure of Christ is characterful and individual, and indicates that the painter was interpreting the story in a very personal way. But though a certain degree of indebtedness to the metropolitan school is to be seen here, the paintings at Boiana are on the whole in a distinct style and represent the work of a highly accomplished local school.

That the metropolitan school exercised an influence elsewhere than in Yugoslavia is shown by paintings which have recently been discovered in the Church of Hagia Sophia at Trebizond, at the far eastern corner of the Black Sea (*Ills. 209–11*). Here the work is in many ways close in style to that at Sopoćani, but the master responsible for the decoration was perhaps more interested in the purely visual side of art, and would seem to have paid considerable attention

209 Christ expels a devil from the daughter of the Canaanite woman – a painting in Hagia Sophia, Trebizond, *c.* 1260. The scene is depicted in a very vivid, expressive manner, and the epileptic fit rendered with almost clinical realism

to living models. In the scene of the Feeding of the Five Thousand, for example, the figures who are assembled in groups to receive their food are all alive and expressive and some would seem to have been inspired by models drawn from the local inhabitants, while no more effective rendering of a person with an epileptic fit has ever been painted than that of the daughter of the Woman of Cana, who lies tense and rigid on the ground while Our Lord causes the devil to depart from her (*Ill. 209*).

Another area of Europe which should undoubtedly also be considered here, if the quality of the paintings is the governing criterion, is Russia. Its art has seldom been taken into account in any general story of developments in Europe and, indeed, it has usually been looked upon as something as far estranged from the story of European art as say the Moslem art of Persia. Yet it was in the direct line of descent from Byzantine art of the Second Golden Age and links between Russia and the Romanesque world were important from the eleventh century onwards, though they were interrupted in

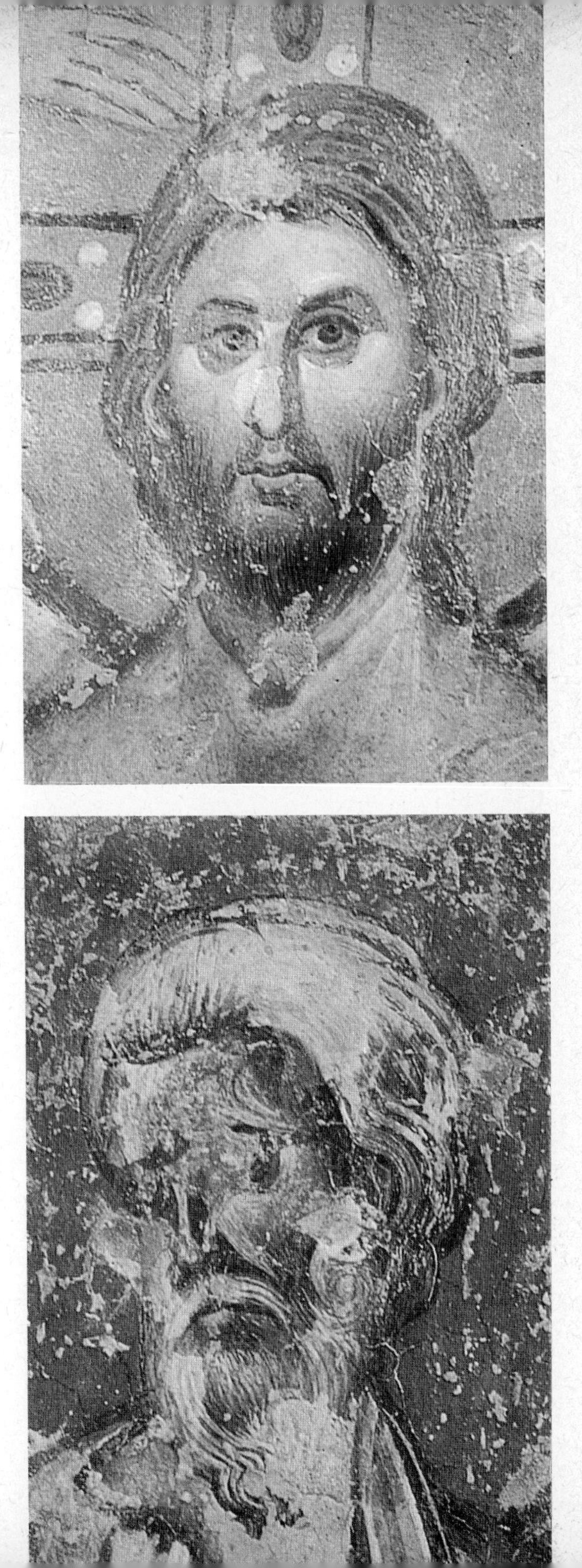

210, 211 Details of paintings in the church of Hagia Sophia, Trebizond, *c.* 1260; Christ (top) and a saint (below). The paintings were outlined on the damp plaster but the modelling was added after it was dry, lighter tones being superimposed on the darker. Often the upper coats have peeled off, but where they are preserved the faces are very fine

212 Four of the daughters of Yaroslav, from Hagia Sophia at Kiev. These paintings already herald the development of a truly Russian style, though some of the other paintings in the building are still essentially Byzantine

the thirteenth century by the Mongol invasions. The group of portraits of members of the family of Yaroslav in Hagia Sophia at Kiev (*Ill. 212*) is significant in this respect, for of his four daughters whose portraits are shown, one was to become queen of Norway, another queen of France and the third queen of Hungary.

The earlier work in Russia, as we have seen was remarkably Byzantine, and even in the twelfth century the Byzantine metropolitan style was to the fore in the painting of the Last Judgement at Vladimir, done *c.* 1195 (*Ill. 201*); hints of this style can be seen at Staraya Ladoga, though the work there is already much more truly Russian than that of Vladimir. The more unconventional paintings that adorned the Church of the Saviour at Nereditsa (*Ill. 213*), near Novgorod, must on the other hand have been inspired to some extent by the art of Syria and Asia Minor. They were executed in 1199 and until the destruction of the church by Hitler's troops during the Second World War they constituted one of the most complete fresco decorations of medieval times to survive. But already the expressiveness of the faces and the attempts at the interpretation of human emotions, combined with a profoundly transcendental outlook, represent the working of racial characteristics which are Russian rather than Greek, and though links with the Byzantine world continued, it would seem that the art of the wall paintings had already by the turn of the century become, to a great extent, a Russian art. In panel painting the change was perhaps even more marked, for the experts would have no great problem in assigning a twelfth-century icon, like the great St Demetrius in the Tretyakov Gallery at Moscow, to a Russian and not to a Byzantine master.

213 Interior of the Church of the Saviour at Nereditsa, Russia, 1199. Until its destruction by Hitler's troops in the Second World War, this was probably the most complete series of wall paintings in Russia or the Byzantine world that survived from the twelfth century

Unfortunately, we know very little about Russian art of the thirteenth century. Paintings of this age exist in the Balkans and in Asia Minor which suggest that the conquest of Constantinople by the Crusaders in 1204 and the occupation of the city by the Latins between then and 1261 was responsible for the exodus of a considerable number of artists who were not ready or not permitted to work for Latin patrons. Such men, one would expect, would also have gone to Russia. But if they did none of their works survive.

The Russian icons we know from this age are mostly already more truly Russian, and the next important series of wall paintings that has come down to us, in the church of the Svetogorsk Monastery, done in 1313, already shows features which were to become usual in Russia towards the end of the fourteenth century. They are thus characterized by sharp, strong highlights, daring experiments in iconography, and a marked search for expression. In the Byzantine world the choice of subject-matter had been very closely controlled by the Church, and though new themes had begun to enter into the repertory in the twelfth century, as we saw at Nerezi, their character was still restricted to events recorded in the Gospels. In Russia wholly new themes, often of an imaginative, abstract character, were being introduced; that of 'Our Lady's Assembly' was one of the most important of them.

Although the attempt to express or interpret ideas was never forsaken, Russian art from the beginning of the fourteenth century was at the same time more abstract and more personal than Byzantine both with regard to style and to its manner of interpretation. Its most outstanding exponent was however a Greek, named Theophanes. He began his life as a painter in Constantinople, but moved to Russia before middle age and developed a style which was more Russian than it was Byzantine; like another great Greek, Domenikos Theotocopoulos (El Greco) some two centuries later, he not only perfected his own style away from his homeland, but also knew how to set free the genius of a nation other than his own.

214 Mosaic of the Marriage Feast of Cana in the church of the Saviour in Chora (Kariye Camii), Constantinople, *c.* 1315. These mosaics have recently been cleaned under the auspices of the Byzantine Institute of America, and the church is now revealed as a jewel of beauty

CONSTANTINOPLE: THE LAST PHASE

These developments round the periphery of the Byzantine world were to culminate in Constantinople soon after the year 1300 with the production of a series of very outstanding church decorations both in mosaic and paint, and in the production, at much the same time, of a number of very outstanding panels. Though the best work was done during the fifty years or so following the year 1300, so that it really falls outside the scope of this book, brief mention may be made of the most important of these works, because they take a place at the end of the long story of Byzantine art rather than at the beginning of that of the new art of the West. Things might have been different had not the Byzantine Empire progressively declined in wealth and importance throughout the fourteenth century, finally to fall before the advance of the Turks in the middle of the fifteenth.

The most important of these later works are the mosaics and paintings that adorn the Church of the Chora at Constantinople, better known by its Turkish name of Kariye Camii (*Ills. 214–17*), executed during the second decade of the fourteenth century. They have recently been very successfully cleaned by specialists working for the Byzantine Institute of America. The church itself and two transverse narthices to the west of it originally contained mosaics depicting a very full series of scenes from the lives of Christ and the Virgin. They are all on a small scale, and if they lack the monumental qualities of the Sopoćani paintings, they make up for this by the elegance and exquisite beauty of the work. The backgrounds are full and elaborate, the scenes animated and brilliant and the colour quite glorious. The technique at times approaches that of the miniature painter, but the technical excellence is manifest, and the effect wholly satisfactory. That the beauty of this decoration is not to be attributed only to the jewel-like quality of the material is proved by the fact that the wall paintings that decorate a chapel which stretches the length of the church on the southern side are no less beautiful (*Ill. 216*).

215 Mosaic in Kariye Camii depicting Joseph's dream and the journey to Bethlehem. Besides the very lively scenes, the decorative borders play a prominent part in the decoration of the church as a whole. The work is very precise, the colouring rich and very lovely

216 Attached to the south side of Kariye Camii is a chapel decorated with wall paintings. The style is closely akin to that of the mosaics, and the work is of very high quality. It was done *c.* 1320. This detail shows the Descent into Hell with Christ raising Adam from the grave

There is evidence to indicate that a great deal of work of this age once existed in Constantinople, but little now survives. There was more at Salonica, and some mosaics in the Church of the Holy Apostles there dating from *c.* 1312 may be noted. Many fine panels or icons were also produced, notably one of the Annunciation from a church at Ochrid in Yugoslavia (*Ill. 218*), but painted at Constantinople. They are paintings of great beauty and deserve to be accorded a more important place in the story of European art than they have hitherto received. More painting of high quality was also executed at Mistra on the Peloponnese, at Ivanovo in Bulgaria and in the monasteries of the Morava Valley in Yugoslavia till these regions were overrun by the Turks in the middle of the fifteenth century. The art that was produced there is all of high quality and comes as a fitting conclusion to the long story of Byzantine painting as it had developed over a period of some twelve hundred years.

217 Opposite: mosaic over the door of Kariye Camii, depicting the donor offering a model of the church to Christ. The donor, Theodore Metochites, was an important court official, but later fell into disgrace and in fact ended his days in the very monastery of which he had been so generous a benefactor

218 Below: one side of a double-sided processional icon from the Peribleptos (St Clement) at Ochrid in Yugoslavia. Painted in Constantinople, the icon was presented to the Bishop of Ochrid early in the fourteenth century

219 The Deesis – Christ between the Virgin and St John – a miniature in the Psalter of Melissenda. The illustrations of this Psalter were executed in the Holy Land at the time of the Crusades and the style shows a mixture of Byzantine and Western influences

CHAPTER ELEVEN

The Gothic world

The style we know as Gothic emerged gradually from Romanesque without any definite break and continued, in the North at least, until well after 1300, which is the point where this book has to end. Gothic Europe was in many ways more united than Romanesque. It also embraced a more extensive area. Already in the twelfth century the horizon of the Western world had begun to extend its bounds in the geographical sense. A growing enthusiasm for pilgrimage had opened up new routes of communication between the countries north of the Alps, Rome and Spain, and by quite early in the twelfth century what we know as the pilgrimage routes were in full operation, conveying large masses of the faithful to Rome on the one hand and Santiago di Compostella in Spain, burial place of the Apostle James, on the other. A kindred motivation was at the basis of the Crusades which were to free Spain from Arab domination during the course of the next century and which already by 1099 had established a Western feudal kingdom in the Holy Land, and set on foot a continual flow of men and materials between the two areas. These events were to have a considerable effect on art. Thanks to the pilgrimage routes across France artistic contacts were established between the more advanced and the more out-of-the-way centres of the West; north-western Spain, hitherto isolated, was brought within the realm of the Romanesque and Gothic art streams and contacts with the Islamic worlds, both in southern Spain and North Africa and in Syria and Egypt, introduced a whole series of new ideas into Western art. They are, it is true, most apparent in the realm of architecture, but painting was not unaffected, for the extended horizons put a great deal of new subject-matter at the painters' disposal while a number of motifs proper to Islamic art were finding their way into Western works. An illumination in a copy of Beatus's Commentary on the Apocalypse now in the Bibliothèque Nationale (Lat. 8878) may be noted in this connexion, for its border takes the form of an inscription in the type of Arabic script known as *kufic*. The fact that the earlier Crusaders had passed through Constantinople on their way eastwards also brought about renewed contacts with the Byzantine world which are clearly attested in art – witness some of the pages of the Winchester Psalter and Bible which we have already noted – while a distinct 'Crusading' school of painting developed in the Holy Land, half Western, half Byzantine in style; its best-known product is probably the Melissenda Psalter in the British Museum (*Ill. 219*), but a number of other manuscripts are known and in the course of the last few years a whole series of panels or icons in the same style have been discovered in St Catherine's Monastery on Mount Sinai.

ART IN A NEW DIMENSION

Even more important was expansion in another direction, that of thought. In the eleventh and twelfth centuries learning had been the preserve of ecclesiastical circles; in the later twelfth, with the foundation of the first universities, it was well on the way to becoming universal. Romanesque art had also been born and developed in the monasteries; Gothic was an art of the cathedrals and cities and patrons and artists alike were not slow to be affected by these changes. Most outstanding among the former was Abbot Suger, whose rebuilding of parts of the Abbey Church of Saint-Denis, finished *c.* 1144, set a new fashion from which there was to be no return. The pointed arches, rib vaults and flying buttresses which were used there, if only in an experimental way, made possible an entirely new type of building, soaring, daring, imaginative, and the great expanses of flat wall which had been characteristic of Romanesque, Carolingian, Byzantine and Early Christian architecture alike, were eliminated. As a result there was little space available for wall paintings; instead there were great expanses of window, and as the desire to depict the Bible scenes or the figures of the saints in no way diminished, the subject-matter of the wall paintings was transferred to the windows, and the art of stained glass was born. It is tempting to suggest that the changes in architecture had another effect also, for by making the interiors

220 The great east window in the cathedral at Poitiers: the Crucifixion. Superb though the windows at Chartres are (see *Ills. 221, 222*), that at Poitiers perhaps excels them in the grandeur of its composition

▶

221 King David: a stained glass window at Chartres, of the early thirteenth century. The development of stained glass was perhaps the greatest contribution of the late Romanesque and early Gothic age to art

222 Opposite: the Nativity, at Chartres. With the change to Gothic architecture in the twelfth century the wall space was reduced and that of the windows enlarged so creating a new form of art, painting on stained glass

▶

light instead of dim, a new idea of brightness soon began to affect art as a whole, more especially the work of the miniature painter, so that as the Gothic Age went forward to a new brilliance, a new lightness of touch was introduced, to reach full fruition in such a manuscript as the famous *Très Riches Heures du Duc de Berry*, illuminated by the Limbourg brothers soon after 1400.

The earliest compositions in stained glass were necessarily conditioned by the shape of the windows, though they were often admirably adapted to their limitations: for instance, the single figures of saints in the narrow windows of Augsburg made *c.* 1130, which are among the earliest examples of medieval glass to have survived. But as the architectural style developed and the windows became larger, the area at the disposal of the stained-glass artist made possible more elaborate compositions, and in the great east window at Poitiers, for example, the space permits the inclusion of several scenes. Christ is shown on the Cross in the centre (*Ill. 220*), with below, on each side of the arms, the Virgin, St John, and the figures of Longinus and Stephaton, with reed and spear; above there are groups of figures who really belong to the scene of the Ascension which occupies the top of the window and here Christ is shown before an oval glory supported by angels. The palette is distinct from that of the Augsburg windows; there a rather staring bright green, pale red and yellow predominate, whereas at Poitiers purple, deep blue and darker green are to the fore, colours of incomparable richness and extreme beauty.

These warmer tones were to become typical of the windows of the thirteenth century, notably of the astonishingly rich series at Chartres (*Ills. 221, 222*). Here there are no less than one hundred and seventy-three windows, varying in date from the three at the west end, which would appear to have been executed *c.* 1160 – they escaped the fire which destroyed most of the cathedral in 1194 – to those in the nave, dating from the middle of the thirteenth century. No such perfect or complete a series is to be found elsewhere, and added to the sculptures of the west, south and north doors, the windows go to form an important part of what is undoubtedly one of the finest artistic complexes in the world, though there are individual windows of the highest quality and most extreme beauty in numerous cathedrals and churches throughout Europe.

Light was regarded in the medieval world as one of the principal expressions of divine power, and nowhere was this power to be sensed with so supreme or such glorious effect as when it formed the medium of the picture, blended in all its varying intensity with the glowing colours of the glass. To the medieval mind there was something especially significant about the windows. 'As the glorious sun penetrates the glass without breaking it, so the word of God, the Light of the Father, passes through the body of the Virgin and then leaves it without undergoing any change', wrote St Bernard of Clairvaux (1090–1153). St Bernard, as leader of the Cistercian Order, disapproved of elaborate decorations, so that it is interesting to find him speaking of stained glass in such a manner. Today such esoteric ideas do not necessarily strike the same chord in our thoughts as they did in the medieval mind, but we can admire the beauties of the glass none the less, and nowhere more so than at Chartres.

In spite of the destruction wrought by Puritan iconoclasts in the seventeenth century, much stained glass still remains in England. That at Canterbury (*Ill. 223*) is perhaps the most important, and if the quantity is much less than at Chartres, the quality is nevertheless of the highest order. There is also much fine glass at York, some of it dating from before 1300. But it is to rather later years that the most magnificent of the English windows, such as the vast east

223 Overleaf: section of an early thirteenth-century window at Canterbury, telling the story of a miraculous cure brought about by water from the shrine of St Thomas. The scenes have to be read from left to right in the following order. Bottom row: a nurse in the service of Sir Jordan Fitzeisulf dies of the plague and is buried; the knight's son, William, dies; a pilgrim arrives with the holy water, which is poured down the boy's throat. Top row: coins vowed as an offering to St Thomas if the boy recovers are placed in his hand; he sits up, cured; St Thomas appears to a leper named Gimp, bidding him warn Sir Jordan of what will happen if he fails to perform his vow. Centre row: the parents come to Gimp, who is able to sit up and deliver the message; but (large centre panel) the vow has not been performed, an elder son now sickens and dies and St Thomas appears armed with a sword above the corpse; finally the vow is accomplished and Sir Jordan pours gold and silver into the saint's tomb

▶

windows at Gloucester and York, must be assigned. Here the polychrome tradition established at Poitiers survives with but little real change, the brilliant reds, blues and greens of the basic glass continuing, though the style of the painting upon it has become more elegant, in accordance with changing tastes. But in the great window at the end of the north transept at York, usually known as 'The Five Sisters', we see glass of quite a different type, almost monochrome in colour and depending on intricate pattern for its appeal.

THE GREAT AGE OF ILLUSTRATION

Wall painting virtually ceased in the larger Gothic churches – because there was no wall on which to paint. But books continued to be produced, in response to an ever-growing demand. Even the austere Cistercians, who eschewed sculpture or architectural decoration, seem in the end to have favoured the work of the scribe and illuminator, and from the end of the twelfth century, if not before, the monastic illuminators even in this strict Order were given special dispensation to execute their work in the daily monastic routine.

As with the Romanesque period it is not always easy to distinguish the French from the English illuminations, for the two countries were of course politically very close. There had, it is true, been a marked decline in the production of manuscripts in France in the mid-twelfth century, which was not paralleled in England, but thanks to the enlightened patronage of St Louis (1226–70) there was a brilliant revival in the thirteenth; indeed good work began again quite early in the century, and the lovely Ingeborg Psalter (*Ill. 226*), illuminated at Paris perhaps as early as 1213, bears witness to it. As the century went on the types of book that were illustrated became more numerous, so that we find missals, breviaries, books of hours, and variants like the *Bible Moralisée* being produced in addition to the manuscripts common in the preceding centuries, like Gospel books and psalters. These books were all comparatively small in size, with the result that the miniatures tended to become less monumental and grand, but more delicate and charming.

224 Crucifixion from the Psalter of Robert de Lindeseye, English, *c.* 1220. Christ's eyes are closed, the head is bowed in death and the body sags in the same way as in later Byzantine and Italian art; the attitudes of St John and the Virgin, however, are rather more mannered than they would have been in the Mediterranean world ▶

Bestiaries and herbals were also frequently illustrated and secular patronage began to play a more important part also; indeed knights, ladies and troubadours came more and more to the fore in society, while the growing influence of the universities, Paris in France, Bologna and Padua in Italy, and soon after Oxford in England, now brought an important new element into the sphere of patronage.

In England, as we have seen, the first half of the twelfth century saw the production of many manuscripts of quite outstanding quality, and an ever-increasing number of scriptoria. The work done in the more out-of-the-way places remained fairly conservative, but that done in London and in the south-east of England developed on lines closely parallel with France. The illuminations rapidly became more ornate, more lavish and more delicate. To the colours which had been most in favour in the twelfth century, gold, blue and pink, were added numerous others, notably scarlet, crimson, green and brown, while the severely straight margins which had

225 Part of a page from the Tenyson Psalter, an English work of the earlier thirteenth century. The subject is the fight between David and Goliath, but this theme is made subservient to the decoration, which now begins to play a more important role

226 Opposite: The Agony in the Garden, a page from the Ingeborg Psalter, done in France *c.* 1213. Christ prays above, with two angels before Him; below, the Apostles sleep in a strange tumbled mass

▶

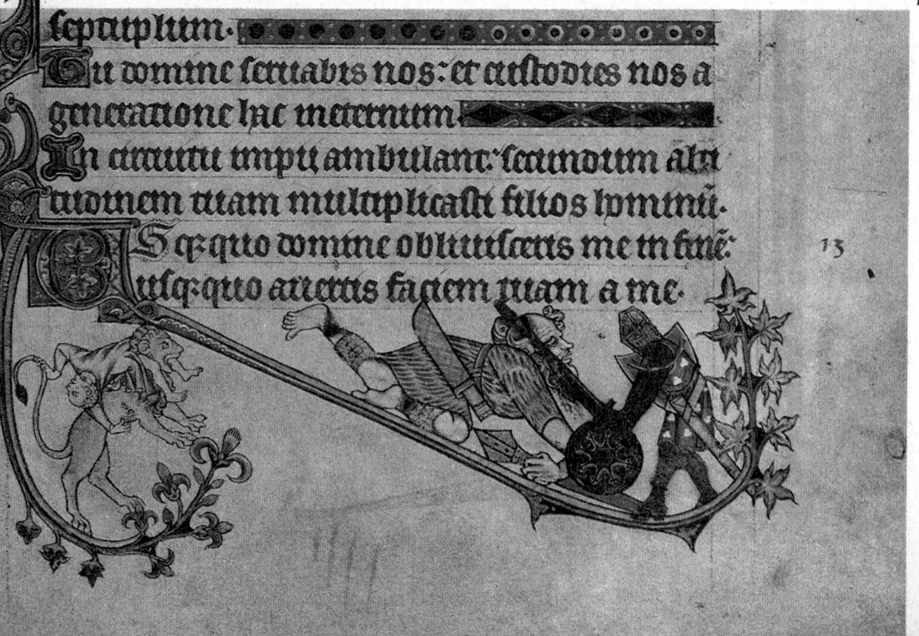

been usual gave place to ones composed of delicate interlace pattern or foliage, while animals and birds were introduced wherever possible. As in France the types of book illustrated became progressively more numerous, though psalters always remained popular – among the finest of them are the Psalter of Robert de Lindeseye, done *c.* 1220 (*Ill. 224*), and the Tenyson Psalter (*Ill. 225*) in the British Museum (Add. 24686), which contains work in two distinct styles, the best of the miniatures dating from *c.* 1280. This book represents the peak of English illumination; thereafter, though the paintings are often enchanting, there is a tendency to sacrifice grandeur to delight. Indeed, in many respects the manuscripts of the later thirteenth century have passed out of what one may call the medieval phase, into one which may be termed that of the age of chivalry, when the delights of this world had become more important than the terrors of the next. The changes towards a greater humanism, which are to be seen in what is really only a rudimentary form in the Mediterranean world, had in the North already moved a long way towards completion.

Though the later twelfth and thirteenth centuries saw great changes in the character and basic nature of art, the position of the artist in society still saw little change. In ancient Greece he had been an individual, known at times by name, and respected for himself, but with the introduction of Christianity, perhaps even before that when new ideas penetrated from the East, his importance as a personality had disappeared. His individuality was eclipsed, to the greater glory of God; his work was anonymous, his position that of a craftsman, and throughout the Byzantine, Carolingian, Ottonian and Romanesque phases hardly a name is recorded. We known that Justinian's architect, who built the great Cathedral of Hagia Sophia at Constantinople, was Anthemius of Tralles, whom a contemporary historian described as 'the man most learned in the mathematical sciences not of this day alone, but of all time'. We also know the name of the sculptor who carved the tympanum at Autun *c.* 1130, Gislebertus; but unless St Dunstan, whom we know of primarily for other things, was himself responsible for the drawing, now in the Bodleian (*Ill. 130*), which shows him prostrated at the feet of Christ, we hardly know the name of a single painter between the Greek Apelles, who painted grapes so well that the birds came to peck them, and Matthew Paris, an Englishman who died *c.* 1250 and executed a number of beautiful line drawings in books. During all these centuries the painter was counted as no more than a craftsman, and had no more claim to personal immortality than a tinker or a tailor. Indeed, even in a census taken in Paris as late as 1323, painters are mentioned along with bakers and clothiers, and they were among the lowest taxed, and therefore the poorest, of the artisan classes. For the change in status of the artist, the close interest in his personality and the beginning of that exalted respect for his gifts which is almost instinctive to us today, we have to go to Italy and to the blossoming of art there in the thirteenth century that was to culminate in what we call the Renaissance.

CHAPTER TWELVE

An end and a beginning

It has become customary to think of Italy as the country of artistic progress and Byzantium as a synonym for conservatism. In the early thirteenth century the roles were exactly reversed. Art in Italy was for the most part arid and didactic. Nothing seems to have been produced that can compare in elegance and accomplishment with the best Byzantine work or in delicacy and charm with what was being done in the Gothic world north of the Alps.

Wall paintings of any real merit are few. Perhaps the most notable are those of Subiaco, the crypt of Anagni (1227–41) and the Church of SS. Quattro Coronati at Rome (*Ill. 228*). They are in a dead desiccated style, of historical rather than artistic interest. Only towards the end of the century are there signs of a growing humanistic approach, as for instance in the frescoes of the Baptistry at Parma, dating from *c.* 1270 (*Ill. 230*). These are very fine, and in a style which can not ineptly be described as 'Proto-Renaissance'.

The 'humanization' of Italian religious art, which some historians have connected with the influence of the Franciscans, comes through with the greatest clarity in the development of crucifix painting. Huge wooden crucifixes, the figures alone often over life-size, hung over the chancels of all great Italian churches, and exercised the talents of the most highly valued artists. The Virgin and St John would normally be shown on either side, and sometimes small scenes would be included, but the main emphasis was naturally on the great, nearly nude figure of Christ. In the earlier examples (*Ill. 231*) He is shown with eyes open and with the body firm and controlled as if

227 Cimabue's great panel known as the *S. Trinità Madonna*, now in the Uffizi Gallery at Florence. It marks a decided step forward in realism (note especially the definition of space in the throne and the facial expressions of the saints at the bottom) as well as being surely one of the grandest panels ever painted

alive – symbol of divine power rather than human suffering – whereas in the later ones (*Ill. 232*) the eyes are closed and the body sags in death, a conception which is far more intimate and personal. The names of several artists painting at this time are known; they include Giunta Pisano (*Ill. 232*), who belonged to an important regional school centred on Pisa; the Berlinghieri family (*Ill. 231*), who worked at Lucca between 1215 and 1275; and Coppo di Marcovaldo, of Florence.

It is at this point, indeed, that art history emerges from anonymity and becomes a matter of real names and reliable documents. The men of the sixteenth century were naturally interested in the originators of the style which they knew – and for this reason the thirteenth-century painters have tended to be regarded as merely 'forerunners' of Giotto, an attitude which does scant justice to their own individuality and genius. In this book, however, the debt that they owe to an old tradition can be appreciated just as much as their role as the precursors of a new phase.

228 Below: painting in the church of the SS. Quattro Coronati at Rome. It depicts Constantine giving the sovereignty of Rome to Pope Sylvester. The style of the work is rather dry and desiccated, representing the least progressive aspect of Romanesque painting in Italy

229 Above: wall painting in the crypt of the cathedral at Aquileia, North Italy: the Deposition. The date of these paintings, which show certain affinities with those at Mileševo, has been disputed, but it is probably to be assigned to shortly before the middle of the thirteenth century

230 The paintings in the Baptistry of Parma, *c.* 1270, form a marked contrast to those in the SS. Quattro Coronati (left). Here there is a new monumentality a new search for humanism, and the work may be described as proto-Renaissance rather than Romanesque

231 Crucifix by the elder Berlinghieri (mid-thirteenth century). Christ is shown alive on the cross, with eyes open and with body erect and rigid. This rendering belongs to an old conception which was giving way to the one shown opposite

232 Crucifix by Giunta Pisano. Christ is now shown with closed eyes and body gently sagging in death, but it is still in many ways an idealized rather than a realistic conception

The two greatest names are without doubt Pietro Cavallini of Rome and Cimabue of Florence. Cavallini's early work was close in style to that of the Byzantine Revival, as the mosaics he did for the apse of S. Maria in Trastevere serve to show (*Ill. 233*). They were done in 1291 and comprise figures of the Virgin and Child, St Peter and St Paul, and a series of scenes from the lives of Christ and the Virgin. The iconography is still wholly Byzantine, but there is a greater preoccupation with depth in the backgrounds than what one would have expected to find in the work of a Byzantine master. Cavallini's work done for S. Paolo fuori le Mura some ten years earlier was no doubt equally conservative. Unfortunately, it has not survived.

Shortly after completing the mosaics of S. Maria in Trastevere Cavallini undertook a very extensive series of paintings in S. Cecilia not far distant. They comprised scenes from the Old and New Testaments on the side walls of the church and a great Last Judgement

233 Mosaic of the Birth of the Virgin on the walls of the apse in S. Maria in Trastevere, Rome. The designer was probably Pietro Cavallini and the date 1291, but it is still very close to a Byzantine model both in style and in iconography

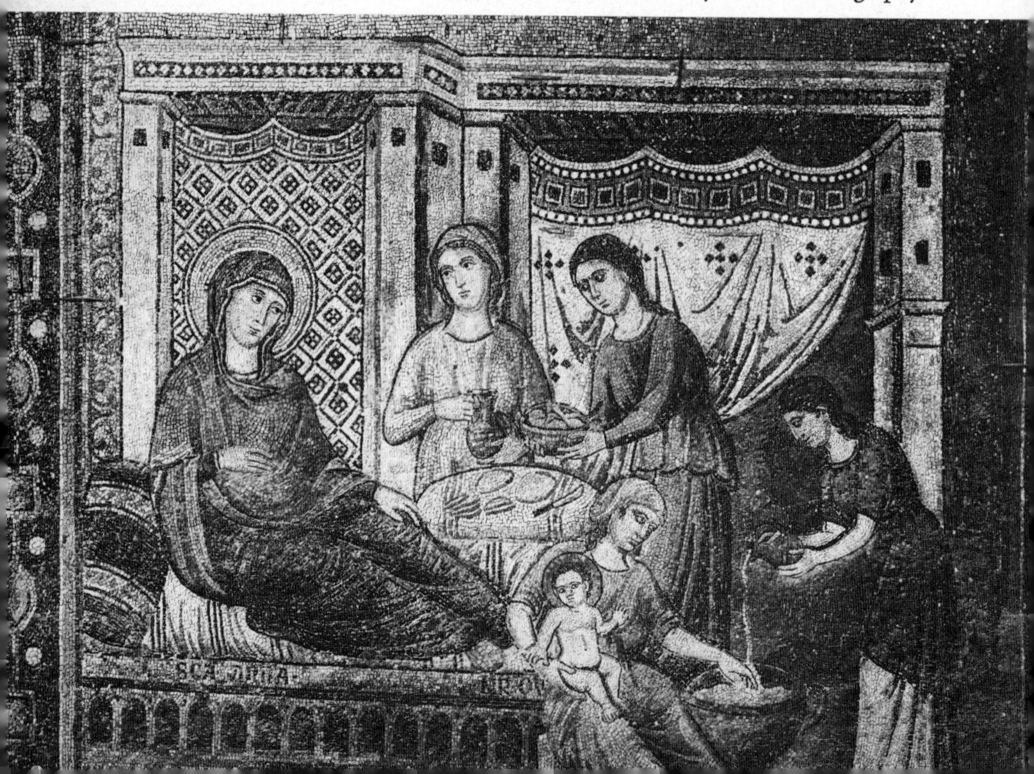

234 Two Apostles from Cavallini's famous painting of the Last Judgement in the church of S. Cecilia, Rome, Cavallini's most important work. The very distinctive faces characterize his personal style, though they have mostly been sadly damaged; but it was the quality of his composition that was to have an even greater effect on his followers

on the western wall; fragments of the latter are now all that remain (*Ills. 234, 235*). They indicate that Cavallini had by this time developed a very personal approach and they show a considerable advance on the mosaics of S. Maria in Trastevere. In S. Cecilia the painter has departed much further from the conventional system of iconography and the modelling, especially that of the drapery, is much more sculpturesque. The colours too are more elaborate and more vivid, and show an infinite gradation. Their brilliant effect is intensified by the black background which the painter favoured. The contours are thick and heavy, but the modelling is accomplished in the old Byzantine manner of using light tones above dark, and also by the extensive use of white highlights. Certain details, like the rendering of the feathers of the angels' wings, also recall Byzantine prototypes. The work not only shows great genius and a marked individuality, but is also essentially progressive. It marks out Cavallini as probably the most important painter working in Italy before 1300.

Vasari ascribed quite a number of other works to this artist, but modern critics are more selective and only accept as definitely by his hand, in addition to those already mentioned, some wall paintings in the Church of S. Maria Donnaregina at Naples, done between 1316 and 1320, and some recently discovered fragments in the Church of S. Maria in Aracoeli at Rome. At Naples, Cavallini worked alongside a number of other men who were rather less distinguished, and only a few individual figures actually represent his work; these are treated in a manner close to that of S. Cecilia, and there seems to have been less change in his style between 1293, when the work in S. Cecilia was done, and 1316, the date of the Naples paintings, than there was between 1291, when the S. Maria in Trastevere mosaics were done, and the paintings of S. Cecilia. Perhaps the greater rigidity of the material, mosaic as opposed to paint, was responsible for this. In any case the mosaics still belong to a medieval, predominantly symbolist trend in art, whereas the paintings pertain to a new style, where moral ideas and their expression have become the painter's main concern. In his paintings Cavallini is thus to be counted just as much an innovator as was Giotto in the north of Italy. At times their work shows a certain similarity, and this is perhaps to be explained as the result of the debt they both owed to Arnolfo di Cambio who was not only known to Giotto in Florence, but who also worked alongside Cavallini in Rome.

The work of the other great genius of this age in Italy, Cimabue, was on the whole rather more conservative than that of Cavallini.

235 St James – a detail from *Ill. 234*. The face has a certain similarity to those of later Byzantine figures of Christ

236 Head of St Francis by Cimabue. The forceful realism of this head contrasts markedly with the more spiritual concept of Cavallini

His frescoes in the Upper Church at Assisi – sad wrecks though they are – are possessed of a monumental grandeur that is absent in Cavallini's art, but they are hardly as progressive, being closer in spirit to Byzantine art of the middle period. Yet there is something majestic about them that puts their painter into the ranks of the very great. They were probably done *c.* 1288. There has been some dispute as to which of the scenes should actually be attributed to him, but recent critics are agreed in accepting as his the figures of the Evangelists in the cross-vaults, together with the scenes of the Apocalypse, the Last Judgement, the Crucifixion and two subjects from the life of St Peter. A Madonna and a painting of St Francis (*Ill. 236*) in the Lower Church are also generally accepted, but they were done rather later, probably in 1295. Earlier, in 1272, Cimabue seems to have been in Rome and he was perhaps also responsible

237, 238 Two paintings that mark a turning-point in the history of art. Left: the *Ruccellai Madonna* by Duccio (1285), one of the formative masterpieces of the school of Siena in the fourteenth and fifteenth centuries, but which still looks back to Byzantine linear sensitivity. Right: the *Ognissanti Madonna* by Giotto (early fourteenth century), standing in the tradition of Cavallini and classical art and pointing forward to Masaccio and the Renaissance ▶

for some of the mosaics in the Baptistry at Florence. A truer idea of his style can be gathered today from the panels than from the frescoes, all of which are in a very poor state of preservation. The earliest of them is a Crucifix at Arezzo, akin to those produced in large numbers by masters of the Pisan school, though Cimabue seems to have been rather more experimental, thus producing more dissonant final results. More distinguished is the great *S. Trinità Madonna* (*Ill. 227*) in the Uffizi at Florence, which was probably

painted *c.* 1285 and is a work of outstanding grandeur. The later *Maestà* in the Louvre, dating perhaps from *c.* 1301, is somewhat paler and less significant, and like the rest of his later work, tends to look rather weak beside that of the more progressive Giotto. Cimabue's paintings really mark the brilliant end of an old phase; Cavallini's indicate the glimmerings of a new one, while it was left to Giotto to establish a wholly new style on a firm footing early in the fourteenth century.

This new style takes us beyond the limits of the present volume. We should, however, remember that it was no sudden, revolutionary change. Art develops, for the most part, by many small modifications, and the great dividing lines (including those used in this book) are wholly arbitrary. We may end, therefore, by merely indicating two lines of progress in the next century, both rooted in the past, both destined to be of crucial significance for the future – the work of two painters who within thirty years of Cimabue's *S. Trinità Madonna* had striven to emulate and surpass him. Giotto in the *Ognissanti Madonna* (*Ill. 238*) gave painting a solidarity, a depth and realism that had not been seen in Europe at least since Roman times; while Duccio in the *Ruccellai Madonna* (*Ill. 237*) treated the same theme with an unparalleled beauty of line and delicacy of composition. In these two we can again detect the same tension between naturalism and abstraction – between representing the outward appearance of the world and creating patterns purely out of the artist's aesthetic sense – which we have seen alternating from the very dawn of art. During the Renaissance the first aspect was to be in the ascendant but, as everything that has happened since serves to prove, that was not the end of the story.

Short Bibliography

Anthony, E. W.	*Romanesque Frescoes*	Princeton	1951
Beckwith, J.	*Early Medieval Art*	London	1964
Grabar, A.	*Byzantine Painting*	Geneva	1953
Grabar, A. and Nordenfalk, C.	*Early Medieval Painting*	Lausanne	1957
	Romanesque Painting	Lausanne	1958
Jantzen, H.	*Ottonische Kunst*	Munich	1947
Koehler, W. R. W.	*Die Karolingischen Miniaturen*	Berlin	1930
Maiuri, A.	*Roman Painting*	Lausanne	1953
Morey, C. R.	*Medieval Art*	New York	1942
Rice, D. Talbot	*The Beginnings of Christian Art*	London	1964
	Art of the Byzantine Era	London	1963
	English Art, 871–1100	Oxford	1952
Robertson, M.	*Greek Painting*	Geneva	1959

List of Illustrations

Measurements are given for the whole picture not details. Inches precede centimetres and height precedes width.

1 Lascaux, Dordogne. Detail of polychrome frieze of horses and bison. *Photo B. Pell.*

2 Altamira, Santander. Deer in red-brown with thin black outline. 89 in. (225 cm.) *Photo B. Pell.*

3 Niaux, Ariège. Bison in black outline with spears. L. of animal 40 in. approx. (100 cm.)

4 La Mouthe, Dordogne. Abstract design in black and red. H. 31½ in. (80 cm.) *Photo B. Pell.*

5 Lascaux, Dordogne. Bison in black and red. L. overall 94½ in. (240 cm.)

6 Lascaux, Dordogne. Great frieze of aurochs, horses and deer in polychrome. L. of aurochs. 156 in. (400 cm.)

7 Lascaux, Dordogne. Black outline painting of wounded bison, 'Man' and bird.

8 Altamira, Santander. Collapsed bison in red with black outline. L. 72 in. (185 cm.) *Photo B. Pell.*

9 Altamira, Santander. Standing bison in red with black outline. L. 77 in. (195 cm.) *Photo B. Pell.*

10 Font de Gaume, Dordogne. Horse in thick black outline on stalactitic background. L. 45 in. (115 cm.) *Photo B. Pell.*

11 New Grange. Detail of spiral decoration. L. 19 in. (48 cm.) *Photo Bord Fáilte Eireann.*

12 Knossos. Wall painting from a small court in the Palace showing bull-game. Shortly after 1500 BC.

13 Agia Triada. Fresco on side of a sarcophagus depicting sacrificial rites. *c.* 1400 BC. L. 54 in. (137 cm.) *Photo Hirmer Archives Munich.*

14 Palaikastro. 'Marine style' two-handled flask. Late 16th century BC. H. 11 in. (28 cm.) Heraklion Museum. *Photo Josephine Powell.*

15 Knossos. Fresco fragment from the Palace depicting a priestess, so-called 'La Parisienne'. *c.* 1500–1450 BC. H. of figure 10 in. (25 cm.) *Photo Hirmer Archives Munich.*

16 Athens. Geometric *krater. c.* 800 BC. H. 22½ in. (57 cm.) Louvre, Paris. *Photo Hirmer Archives Munich.*

17 Argos. Argive *krater* fragment depicting Polyphemus and Odysseus. Mid 7th century BC. Argos Museum. *Photo French School, Athens.*

18 Kameiros, Rhodes. Early Corinthian *olpe* with snake, lions and winged beasts. Late 7th century BC. H. 11½ in. (29 cm.) British Museum, London. *Photo Hirmer Archives Munich.*

19 Athens. Black-figure amphora by Exekias. Detail showing the murder of Penthesilea by Achilles. *c.* 540 BC. British Museum, London. *Photo Hirmer Archives Munich.*

20 Athens. Clay plaque from the Acropolis, probably by Euthymides. *c.* 500 BC. W. 20 in. (51 cm.) Acropolis Museum, Athens. *Photo German Archaeological Institute, Athens.*

21 Athens. Red-figure amphora by the Berlin Painter. Detail with Hermes and a satyr. *c.* 490 BC. Antikenabteilung, Staatliche Museen, Berlin. *Photo Hirmer Archives Munich.*

22 Athens. White-ground lekythos by the Phiale Painter. Seated woman. 440–430 BC. H. 17 in. (37 cm.) Museum Antiker Kleinkunst, Munich. *Photo Hirmer Archives Munich.*

23 Athens. White-ground cup by the Pistoxenos painter. Aphrodite riding a goose. *c.* 470 BC. Diam. 9½ in. (24 cm.) British Museum, London.

24 Greek vase painting by Asteas. 'Miser and thieves'. 360–330 BC. Antikenabteilung, Staatliche Museen, Berlin.

25 Pompeii. Mosaic depicting the Battle of the Issus, from the House of the Faun. Before AD 79, from original Greek painting of *c.* 330 BC. 107 in. × 201 in. (271 × 512 cm.) Museo Nazionale, Naples. *Photo Alfredo Foglia.*

26 Pella. Pebble-mosaic showing a stag hunt. *c.* 300 BC.

27 Kazanlik. Detail of wall painting in tomb vault showing men and horses. *Photo D. P. Dimitrov.*

28 Pompeii. Mosaic with 'Nilotic' scene. Before AD 79. Museo Nazionale, Naples. *Photo Scala.*

29 Taranto. Fragment of *krater* with stage scenery and figures. Mid 4th century BC. Martin von Wagner Museum der Universität, Würzburg.

30 Stabiae. Wall painting with harbour scene. Before AD 79. 9½ × 10½ in. (24 × 27 cm.) Museo Nazionale, Naples. *Photo André Held.*

31 Near Pompeii. Wall painting of romantic landscape from the Villa of Agrippa Posthumus. Before AD 79. 61¼ × 39¼ in. (156 × 100 cm.) Museo Nazionale, Naples. *Photo André Held.*

32 Pompeii. Wall painting of the 'Three Graces'. 22½ × 22½ in. (57 × 57 cm.) Museo Nazionale, Naples. *Photo André Held.*

33 Tarquinia. Wall painting in the Tomb of the Leopards. Banqueters. *c.* 470 BC.

34 Tarquinia. Wall painting in the Tomb of the Baron. Detail of youth on horseback. 41¼ × 14 in. (105 × 35 cm.)

35 Tarquinia. Wall painting in the Tomb of the Shields. Funerary banquet with Velthur Velcha and his wife. 3rd century BC.

36 Prima Porta, near Rome. Wall painting of the 'Garden of Livia'. Late 1st century BC. H. of wall 118 in. (300 cm.) Museo delle Terme, Rome. *Photo Georgina Masson.*

37 Pompeii. Wall painting of still life with fruit bowl and amphora, from the House of Julia Felix. Before AD 79. 35¼ × 48 in. (89·5 × 122 cm.) Museo Nazionale, Naples. *Photo Alfredo Foglia.*

38 Pompeii. Wall painting of Perseus and Andromeda, from the House of Dioscorides. Before AD 79, after original Greek painting of 4th century BC. Museo Nazionale, Naples. *Photo André Held.*

39 Pompeii. Mosaic with strolling players by Dioscourides of Samos, from the Villa of Cicero. Museo Nazionale, Naples. *Photo André Held.*

40 Herculaneum. Wall painting, transferred to panel, of a tragic actor. 15¾ × 15¾ in. (40 × 40 cm.) Museo Nazionale, Naples. *Photo André Held.*

41 Rome. Detail from a wall painting depicting a wedding ceremony, the 'Aldobrandini Wedding'. 1st century AD. Musei e Gallerie Pontificie, Vatican. *Photo Scala.*

42 The Fayum, Egypt. Portrait of a man. Encaustic on wood. 2nd century AD. H. 15 in. (38 cm.) Rogers Fund, Metropolitan Museum of Art, New York.

43 Pompeii. Painting of Terentius Neo and his wife (?). 23½ × 20½ in. (59·7 × 52 cm.) Museo Nazionale, Naples. *Photo André Held.*

44 Herculaneum. Wall painting with fourth style scenographic decoration. Shortly before AD 79. Museo Nazionale, Naples. *Photo Scala.*

45 Rome. Wall painting in Chamber III of the Hypogeum of the Aurelians. Head of an Apostle. Mid 3rd century. 6½ × 4½ in. (16·5 × 11·5 cm.) *Photo Gabinetto Fotografico Nazionale.*

46 Rome. Wall painting in the Catacomb of Priscilla. Balaam pointing out the Star to Mary. 3rd century. 16 × 10½ in. (40·7 × 26·6 cm.) *Photo André Held.*

47 Rome. Wall painting in the Catacomb of Domitilla. Jesus as the Good Shepherd. 3rd century. 20×36 in. (50·8×91·5 cm.) *Photo André Held.*

48 Rome. Wall painting in the Catacomb of Callixtus. Moses striking the rock. 4th century. 26×46 in. (66×94 cm.) *Photo Hirmer Archives Munich.*

49 Rome. Wall painting in the Capella Greca, Catacomb of Priscilla. Three Hebrews in the Fiery Furnace. Early 4th century. 20×34½ in. (50·8×87·5 cm.) *Photo Hirmer Archives Munich.*

50 Constantinople. Detail of mosaic floor of the Great Palace. 6th century. *Photo Walker Trust*

51 Piazza Armerina, Sicily. Detail of mosaic in the 'Room of the Ten Girls' in the Imperial villa. Late 3rd century.

52 Zliten, Tripolitania. Mosaic of birds in a nest. Probably AD 200. Castello Museum, Tripoli. *Photo Roger Wood.*

53 Zliten, Tripolitania. Mosaic of threshing scene. Probably AD 200. Castello Museum, Tripoli. *Photo Roger Wood.*

54 Constantinople. Detail from the border of the mosaic floor of the Great Palace. 6th century. *Photo Walker Trust.*

55 Dura Europos. Wall painting in the temple of the Palmyrene gods. 'Sacrifice of Conon'. 1st century AD. Damascus Museum. *Photo courtesy of Direction Générale des Antiquités et des Musées, Damascus.*

56 Ravenna. Mosaic of procession of female saints in S. Apollinare Nuovo. AD 561. *Photo Mansell/Alinari.*

57 Rome. Detail of vault mosaic in Sta Costanza. Vintaging scene. Early 4th century. *Photo Mansell/Alinari.*

58 Ravenna. Apse mosaic in S. Vitale. Empress Theodora and her attendants. Church consecrated AD 547. *Photo Hirmer Archives Munich.*

59 Ravenna. Mosaic panel in nave of S Apollinare Nuovo. Christ dividing Sheep and Goats. *c.* AD 500–26. *Photo Hirmer Archives Munich.*

60 Rome. Mosaic in nave of Sta Maria Maggiore. Jacob negotiates the land when he has pitched his tent. Second quarter of 5th century. *Photo Scala.*

61 Ravenna. Dome of the Baptistry of the Orthodox. *c.* AD 440. *Photo Hirmer Archives Munich.*

62 Ravenna. Mosaic lunette in Mausoleum of Galla Placidia. Christ as the Good Shepherd. Mid 5th century. *Photo Hirmer Archives Munich.*

63 Rome. Apse mosaic in SS Cosmas and Damian. Christ in Glory AD 526–30. *Photo Scala.*

64 Ravenna. Apse mosaic in S. Vitale. Christ enthroned between St Vitale and St Ecclesias and two angels. Mid 6th century. *Photo Hirmer Archives Munich.*

65 Salonica. Apse mosaic in Church of Hosios David. Detail of Christ in Glory. Mid 5th century. *Photo Hirmer Archives Munich.*

66 Salonica. Mosaic frieze in the dome of Church of St George. Two saints in architectural setting AD 400. *Photo Hirmer Archives Munich.*

67 Codex Vergilius Romanus. Shepherds tending their flocks. Late 4th century. 8⅝×8¾ in. (21·9×22·2 cm.) Vatican Library (Vat. Lat. 3867 f.44r.)

68 Codex Sinopensis. Christ healing two blind men of Jericho. 6th century. 11¾×9¾ in. (29·8×24·8 cm.) Bibliothèque Nationale, Paris (Suppl. gr. 1286 f.29.)

69 Vienna Genesis. Eliezer and Rebecca's Parents. 5th century. 12¼×9¾ in. (31·1×24·8 cm.) Nationalbibliothek, Vienna (Vindob. theol. gr. 31 f.7.)

70 Rossano Gospels. The Entry into Jerusalem. 6th century. 12×10¼ in. (30·7×26 cm.) Museo Diocesano, Rossano (Folio 11.) *Photo Hirmer Archives Munich.*

71 Rome. Wall painting in a niche in the atrium of S. Maria Antiqua. St Abbacyr the Physician. 7th century. *Photo André Held.*

72 Rome. Wall painting near the apse of S. Maria Antiqua. Fragment of an Annunciation with head of an angel. 6th–7th century. *Photo de Antonis.*

73 Rome. Mosaic vault in S. Zeno Chapel, S. Prassede. Detail of angel supporting central roundel. 9th century. *Photo Scala.*

74 Rome. Wall painting in S. Maria Antiqua. The Crucifixion. *Photo Gabinetto Fotografico Nazionale.*

75 Salonica. Mosaic in the Church of St Demetrius. St Demetrius between Bishop John and Leontius. *c.* AD 640. *Photo Hirmer Archives Munich.*

76 Salonica. Mosaic in the Church of St Demetrius. St Demetrius and two children. *c.* AD 640. *Photo Hirmer Archives Munich.*

77 Mt. Sinai. Apse mosaic in the Monastery of St Catherine. The Transfiguration. *c.* AD 565. *Photo Roger Wood.*

78 Mt. Sinai. Icon from the Monastery of St Catherine. The Crucifixion. 7th century. $18\frac{1}{4}\times 10$ in. ($46{\cdot}4\times 25{\cdot}5$ cm.) *Photo Allen.*

79 Mt. Sinai. Icon from the Monastery of St Catherine. Virgin and Child enthroned between saints and archangels. Encaustic painting. 6th century. $27\frac{1}{2}\times 17\frac{3}{4}$ in. (70×45 cm.) *Photo Institut Français d'Athènes.*

80 Mt. Sinai. Icon from the monastery of St Catherine. Three Hebrews in the Fiery Furnace, an angel beside them. 6th century. $13\frac{3}{8}\times 19\frac{5}{8}$ in. (34×50 cm.) *Photo Allen.*

81 Mt. Sinai. Icon from the Monastery of St Catherine. St Peter. Encaustic painting. 6th century. $20\frac{1}{2}\times 15\frac{3}{8}$ in. (52×39 cm.) *Photo Institut Français d'Athènes.*

82 Rome. Virgin and Child, in S. Francesco Romana, Rome. Panel painting. 7th century. *Photo Josephine Powell.*

83 Castelseprio. Wall painting in S. Maria Foris Portas. The Nativity and Annunciation to the Shepherds. 8th–9th century. *Photo Hirmer Archives Munich.*

84 Castelseprio. Wall painting in S. Maria Foris Portas. Presentation in the Temple. 8th–9th century. *Photo Hirmer Archives Munich.*

85 South Italian (?). The Scribe Ezra, prefixed to Northumbrian Bible. Late 6th century. $19\frac{3}{8}\times 13$ in. ($49{\cdot}1\times 33{\cdot}1$ cm.) Biblioteca Medicea Laurenziana, Florence (Codex Amiatinus I f.v.)

86 Lindisfarne. St Matthew, from the Lindisfarne Gospels. AD 698–721. $13\frac{1}{2}\times 9\frac{3}{4}$ in. ($34{\cdot}4\times 24{\cdot}8$ cm.) British Museum, London (Cotton MS. Nero D.iv. f.25v.)

87 Lindisfarne. Ornamental page, from the Lindisfarne Gospels. AD 698–721. $13\frac{1}{2}\times 9\frac{3}{4}$ in. ($34{\cdot}4\times 24{\cdot}8$ cm.) British Museum, London (Cotton MS. Nero D.iv. f.26 v.) *Photo Eileen Tweedy.*

88 Lindisfarne. Detail of ornamental initial, from the Lindisfarne Gospels. AD 698–721. British Museum, London (Cotton MS. Nero D.iv. f.3.)

89 Ireland. The Temtation of Christ, from the Book of Kells 9th century. Trinity College Library, Dublin (Folio 202v.) *Photo by courtesy of the Board of Trinity College.*

90 Hiberno-Saxon. Symbol of St Matthew, from the Book of Durrow. Second half of 7th century. $9\frac{5}{8}\times 6\frac{1}{8}$ in. ($21{\cdot}9\times 15{\cdot}5$ cm.) Trinity College Library, Dublin (MS.A.4.5 f.245v.) *Photo by courtesy of the Board of Trinity College.*

91 Ireland. Virgin and Child, from the Book of Kells. 9th century. Trinity College Library, Dublin. *Photo by courtesy of the Board of Trinity College.*

92 Merovingian. Illumination from the Sacramentary of Gelasius. AD 750–70. Biblioteca Apostolica Vaticana.

93 Germigny-des-Prés. Mosaic in the Oratory of Theodulf. The Ark of the Covenant. AD 799–818. *Photo Thames and Hudson Archives.*

94 Auxerre. Wall painting in the upper crypt of the Church of St Germain. Martyrdom of St Stephen. 9th century. *Photo Archives Photographiques.*

95 Müstair. Wall painting in the Church of St John the Baptist. Christ healing the Dumb. Early 9th century.

96 Palace School, Aachen. St Matthew, from the Gospels of Charlemagne. Before AD 800. Kunsthistorisches Museum, Vienna (Folio 15.)

97 Palace School, Aachen. The Four Evangelists, from a Gospel Book. Early 9th century. Cathedral Treasury, Aachen. *Photo Bildarchiv Foto Marburg.*

98 Palace School, Aachen. The Fountain of Life, from the Evangelistary of Godescalc. AD 781–3. $12\times 8\frac{1}{4}$ in. ($30{\cdot}5\times 21$ cm.) Bibliothèque Nationale, Paris (MS. Lat. 1203 f.3v.)

99 Palace School, Aachen. Christ blessing, from the Evangelistary of Godescalc. AD 781–3. $12\times 8\frac{1}{4}$ in. ($30{\cdot}5\times 21$ cm.) Bibliothèque Nationale, Paris (MS. Lat. 1203 f.3r.)

100 Trier. Ornamental initial, from the Gospel Book of Trier. Stadtbibliothek Trier (MS. 23 f.63v.) *Photo Bildarchiv Foto Marburg.*

101 Hautvillers, near Rheims. St Matthew, from the Gospel Book of Archbishop Ebbo of Rheims. Between 816 and 835. $10\frac{3}{16}\times 7\frac{13}{16}$ in. ($25{\cdot}9\times 19{\cdot}9$ cm.) Bibliothèque Nationale, Paris (MS. 1 f.18v.)

102 Tours. Monks from the Abbey of St Martin at Tours, headed by their lay abbot, Count Vivian, presenting the Bible to King Charles the Bald, from Count Vivian's Bible. AD 843–51. $19\frac{3}{8}\times 14\frac{5}{8}$ in. ($49{\cdot}5\times 37{\cdot}5$ cm.) Bibliothèque Nationale, Paris (MS. Lat. I f.423v.)

103 Court School of Charles the Bald, Tours. Christ enthroned with Evangelists and Great Prophets, from the Codex Aureus of St Emmeram. *c.* AD 870. Staatsbibliothek, Munich (Cod. 14000 f.6v.) *Photo Hirmer Archives Munich.*

104 Tours. Portrait of Emperor Lothair I, from the Gospels of Lothair. AD 849–51. $12\frac{5}{8}\times 9\frac{3}{4}$ in. ($32{\cdot}1\times 24{\cdot}8$ cm.) Bibliothèque Nationale, Paris (MS. Lat. 266 f.1v.)

105 Rheims. Illustration of Psalm CXI (112), from the Utrecht Psalter. *c.* AD 832. $12\frac{7}{8}\times 9\frac{7}{8}$ in. ($32{\cdot}7\times 25{\cdot}1$ cm.) Bibliothek der Rijksuniversiteit, Utrecht.

106 Rheims. Illustration of Psalm XXVI (27), from the Utrecht Psalter. *c.* AD 832. $12\frac{7}{8}\times 8\frac{7}{8}$ in. ($32{\cdot}7\times 25{\cdot}1$ cm.) Bibliothek der Rijksuniversiteit, Utrecht.

107 Galliano. Wall painting in the Church of S. Vincenzo. The Prophet Jeremiah, *c.* AD 1007.

108 Reichenau, Oberzell. Wall painting in the Church of St Georg. The Raising of Lazarus. 10th century. *Photo Staatliches Amt für Denkmalspflege, Karlsruhe.*

109 Reichenau or Trier. The Massacre of the Innocents, from the Codex Egberti. *c.* AD 985. Stadtbibliothek Trier. (Codex 24.) *Photo Bildarchiv Foto Marburg.*

110 Regensburg. The Crucifixion, from the Gospel Book of Abbess Uota of Niedermünster. AD 1002–25. $15\times 10\frac{5}{8}$ in. (38×27 cm.) Staatsbibliothek, Munich (Clm. 13601 f.3v. & 4r.) *Photo Hirmer Archives Munich.*

111 Reichenau or Court School of Otto III. The Entry into Jerusalem, from the Gospel Book of Otto III. AD 996–1002. $13\times 9\frac{3}{8}$ in. ($33\times 23{\cdot}8$ cm.) Staatsbibliothek, Munich (Clm. 4453 f.234v.) *Photo Hirmer Archives Munich.*

112 Reichenau or Court School of Otto III. Personifications of the four chief provinces, Slavinia, Germania, Gallia and Rome, paying homage to Otto III. From the Gospel Book of Otto III. AD 996–1002. $13\times 9\frac{3}{8}$ in. ($33\times 23{\cdot}8$ cm.) Staatsbibliothek, Munich (Clm. 4453 f.23r.) *Photo Hirmer Archives Munich.*

113 Cologne. The Marriage of Cana, from the Hitda Gospel Book. *c.* AD 1010.

$11\frac{3}{8}\times 8\frac{5}{8}$ in. (29×22 cm.) Hessische Landes- und Hochschulbibliothek, Darmstadt (Hs. 1640 f.169.) *Photo Bildarchiv Foto Marburg.*

114 Reichenau or Court School of Henry II. The Ascension, from Henry II's Book of Pericopes. AD 1002–14. $10\frac{3}{8}\times 7\frac{1}{2}$ in. (26·4×19 cm.) Staatsbibliothek, Munich (Clm. 4452 f.131v.)

115 Reichenau (?). Initial V, from the Gero Codex. *c.* AD 969. $11\frac{3}{4}\times 8\frac{3}{4}$ in. (29·7×22 cm.) Hessisches Landes- und Hochschulbibliothek, Darmstadt (Hs. 1948 f.117v.) *Photo Bildarchiv Foto Marburg.*

116 School of Echternach. St John, from the Codex Aureus Epternacencis. *c.* AD 1024. Germanisches Nationalmuseum, Nürnberg (Folio 224.)

117 School of Echternach. Christ in Majesty adored by the Emperor Conrad II and the Empress Gisela, from the Codex Aureus of Speyer. AD 1045–6. $19\frac{5}{8}\times 13\frac{3}{4}$ in. (50×35 cm.) Escorial Library, Madrid (Codex Vitrinas 17 f.2v.)

118 Winchester. Edgar offering Charter to Christ, from the New Minster Charter. AD 966. $8\frac{1}{8}\times 6\frac{3}{4}$ in. (20·6×17·1 cm.) British Museum, London (MS. Cotton Vesp. A. viii f.2v.)

119 Winchester. The Three Maries at the Sepulchre, from the Benedictional of St Aethelwold. *c.* AD 975–80. $11\frac{1}{2}\times 8\frac{1}{2}$ in. (29·2×21·6 cm.) British Museum, London (MS. Add. 49598.)

120 Winchester. The Presentation in the Temple, from the Benedictional of St Aethelwold. *c.* AD 975–80. $11\frac{1}{2}\times 8\frac{1}{2}$ in. (29·2×21·6 cm.) British Museum, London (MS. Add. 49598 f.34v.)

121 Canterbury (?). St Matthew, from a Gospel Book. Early 11th century. $12\frac{3}{4}\times 9\frac{1}{4}$ in. (32·5×23·5 cm.) Trinity College Library, Cambridge (MS.B. 10.4.)

122 Winchester. St John the Evangelist, from the Grimbald or New Minster Gospels. Early 11th century. $12\frac{3}{4}\times 9\frac{3}{4}$ in. (35×24·7 cm.) British Museum, London (MS. Add. 34890 f.114v.)

123 Winchester. The Three Maries at the Sepulchre, from the Benedictional of Robert of Jumièges. *c.* AD 900–1037. $12\frac{5}{8}\times 9\frac{1}{8}$ in. (32·2×23·1 cm.) Bibliothèque Publique, Rouen (MS.Y.7.)

124 Winchester (?). The Adoration of the Magi, from the Sacramentary of Robert of Jumièges. *c.* AD 1000. $13\frac{1}{4}\times 8\frac{3}{4}$ in. (33·5×22·2 cm.) Bibliothèque Publique, Rouen (MS.Y.6.)

125 Winchester (?). Pentecost, from the Sacramentary of Robert of Jumièges. *c.* AD 1000. $13\frac{1}{4}\times 8\frac{3}{4}$ in. (33·5×22·2 cm.) Bibliothèque Publique, Rouen (MS.Y.6.)

126 Canterbury (?). The beginning of St Matthew, from Dunstan Gospels. Early 11th century. $13\frac{1}{4}\times 10\frac{3}{4}$ in. (33·5×27·3 cm.) British Museum, London (MS. Roy.I D.ix.)

127 Croyland or Ely (?). Christ Triumphant from a calendar. Second quarter of 11th century. $10\frac{1}{2}\times 6\frac{1}{2}$ in. (26·6×16·5 cm.) Bodleian Library, Oxford (MS. Douce 296 f.40.)

128 Place of origin unknown. St Mark, from York Gospel Book. *c.* AD 1000. York Minster Library. *Photo Courtesy the Dean and Chapter of York.*

129 Hereford (?). St Luke, from the Hereford Gospels. Mid 11th century. $7\frac{3}{4}\times 4$ in. (19·7×10·2 cm.) Pembroke College Library, Cambridge (MS. 302 f.60v.)

130 Glastonbury (?). Christ and St Dunstan, prefixed to Composite Volume. AD 960. $9\frac{3}{4}\times 7\frac{1}{4}$ in. (24·8×18·4 cm.) Bodleian Library, Oxford (MS. Auct. F.4.32 f.1.)

131 Canterbury. Personification of Philosophy. Trinity College Library, Cambridge (MS. 0.3.7.) *Photo courtesy the Master and Fellows of Trinity College, Cambridge.*

132 Canterbury. Illustration to Psalm XVI (17), from a copy of the Utrecht Psalter. *c.* AD 1000. British Museum, London (MS. Harley 603.)

133 Canterbury. Illustration to Psalm XV (16), from the Eadwine Psalter. *c.* AD 1150. Miniature $5\frac{1}{2}\times 11\frac{1}{2}$ in. ($14\times 29{\cdot}2$ cm.) Trinity College Library, Cambridge (MS. R.17.I f.24.) *Photo courtesy the Master and Fellows of Trinity College, Cambridge.*

134 Canterbury. The Fall of the Rebel Angels, from the Caedmon Manuscript. Early 11th century. Bodleian Library, Oxford (MS. Junius II, p. 16.)

135 Winchester. The Last Judgement, from the New Minster *Liber Vitae.* AD 1020–30. $10\frac{1}{8}\times 5\frac{3}{4}$ in. ($25{\cdot}7\times 13{\cdot}6$ cm.) British Museum, London (MS. Stowe 944.)

136 Nicaea. Mosaic of the Virgin, in the Church of the Assumption. 9th century. *Photo Klougé.*

137 Nicaea. Mosaic in the Church of the Assumption. Archangels Arche and Dynamis. 8th century. *Photo Klougé.*

138 Constantinople. Apse mosaic in Hagia Sophia. Virgin and Child. AD 867. *Photo The Byzantine Institute, Inc.*

139 Vault mosaic before the apse in Hagia Sophia. Detail of an archangel. *c.* 867. *Photo Dumbarton Oaks Field Committee.*

140 Nicaea. Mosaic in the Church of the Assumption. Archangel Dynamis (detail of ill. 137). Probably 8th century. *Photo Klougé.*

141 Byzantine. Illumination from the Theriaca of Nicandor. 10th or 11th century. Bibliothèque Nationale, Paris (MS. Suppl. Gr. 247 f.47v.)

142 Byzantine. David composing the Psalms, from the Paris Psalter. Early 10th century. $14\frac{1}{8}\times 10\frac{1}{4}$ in. (36×26 cm.) Bibliothèque Nationale, Paris (MS. Gr. 139.) *Photo Hirmer Archives Munich.*

143 Byzantine. The stoning of Achan, from the Joshua Roll. s. AD 730–843. Vatican Library (MS. Gr. 431.)

144 Byzantine. The Prayer of Isaiah, from the Paris Psalter. Early 10th century. $14\frac{1}{8}\times 10\frac{1}{4}$ (36×26 cm.) Bibliothèque Nationale, Paris (MS. Gr. 139.) *Photo Hirmer Archives Munich.*

145 Byzantine. Moses on Mount Sinai, from the Bible of Leo the Patrician. 10th century. Vatican Library (MS. Reg. Gr. 1.)

146 Byzantine. Raising of Lazarus and Entry into Jerusalem, from the Homilies of St Gregory Nazianzus. 880–883. $16\frac{1}{8}\times 11\frac{3}{4}$ in. ($41\times 30{\cdot}5$ cm.) Bibliothèque Nationale, Paris. *Photo Hirmer Archives Munich.*

147 Byzantine. The Vision of Ezekiel, from the Homilies of St Gregory Nazianzus. 880–883. $61\frac{1}{8}\times 11\frac{3}{4}$ in. ($41\times 30{\cdot}5$ cm.) Bibliothèqie Nationale, Paris. *Photo Hirmer Archives Munich.*

148 Byzantine. Six scenes from the life of David, from the Psalter of Basil II. AD 976–1025. $15\frac{1}{2}\times 11\frac{3}{4}$ in. ($39{\cdot}5\times 30{\cdot}5$ cm.) The Marcian Library, Venice. *Photo Hirmer Archives Munich.*

149 Byzantine. Portrait of Basil II, from the Psalter of Basil II. AD 976–1025. $15\frac{1}{2}\times 11\frac{3}{4}$ in. ($39{\cdot}5\times 30{\cdot}5$ cm.) The Marcian Library, Venice. *Photo Hirmer Archives Munich.*

150 Byzantine. Conception of the World, from the Cosmas Indicopleustes. 9th-century copy of 6th-century original. Vatican Library (MS. Gr. 699 f.43.)

151 Byzantine. Iconoclast whitewashing an image, from the Khludov Psalter. Public Library, Moscow. *Photo École Pratique des Hautes Études, Paris.*

152 Byzantine. The Anointing of David, from a Psalter. AD 1066. British Museum, London (MS. Add. 19352 f.106.)

153 Greece. Apse mosaic in the Monastery Church of Hosios Lukas. Virgin and Child. *c.* AD 1000. *Photo R. Clogg.*

154 Greece. Narthex mosaic in the Monastery Church of Hosios Lukas. The Crucifixion. *c.* AD 1000. *Photo Josephine Powell.*

155 Greece. Mosaic in the Monastery Church of Hosios Lukas. The Nativity. *c.* AD 1000. *Photo Josephine Powell.*

156 Nicaea. Mosaic in the Church of the Assumption. St Mark. *c.* AD 1065. *Photo Klougé*

157 Chios. Mosaic in the Church of Nea Moni. The Anastasis (detail). AD 1042–56. *Photo Rosemary Pierer.*

158 Near Athens. Mosaic in the Church of Daphni. The Transfiguration. *c.* AD 1090. *Photo Josephine Powell.*

159 Near Athens. Mosaic in the Church of Daphni. The Annunciation. *c.* AD 1090. *Photo Josephine Powell.*

160 Near Athens. Mosaic in the Church of Daphni. A Prophet. *c.* AD 1090. *Photo Josephine Powell.*

161 Near Athens. Mosaic in the Church of Daphni. The Crucifixion (detail). *c.* AD 1090. *Photo Josephine Powell.*

162 Near Athens. Mosaic in the Church of Daphni. The Annunication to Anna. *c.* AD 1090. *Photo Josephine Powell.*

163 Near Athens. Dome mosaic in the Church of Daphni. Christ the Almighty *c.* AD 1090. *Photo the author.*

164 Ochrid. Wall painting on western wall of Church of Hagia Sophia. Detail of Christ from the Dormition of the Virgin. *c.* AD 1050. After Raška.

165 Constantinople. Mosaic above narthex door of Hagia Sophia. Leo VI before Christ. AD 886–912. 185×90½ in. (470×230 cm.) *Photo courtesy of the Byzantine Institute, Inc.*

166 Constantinople. Mosaic above south door of Hagia Sophia. Constantine and Justinian offering homage to the Virgin. *c.* AD 986–94. 194½×118⅞ in. (494×302 cm.) *Photo Hirmer Archives Munich.*

167 Detail of plate 165.

168 Constantinople. South gallery mosaic in Hagia Sophia. Christ blessing the Empress Zoe and Constantine Monomachos. AD 1042–55. Original height 96⅛×94½ in. (244×240 cm.) *Photo Hirmer Archives Munich.*

169 Detail of plate 166.

170 Constantinople. Mosaic in Hagia Sophia. Virgin and Child between Emperor John Comnenus and the Empress Irene. *c.* AD 1118. *Photo Hirmer Archives Munich.*

171 Palermo. Mosaic in the Church of the Martorana. The Nativity. AD 1143–51. *Photo Mansell/Anderson.*

172 Monreale, Mosaic in the Cathedral. Esau hunting (detail). AD 1180–90.

173 Detail of plate 174.

174 Constantinople. Mosaic in Hagia Sophia. The Deesis. Mid 12th century. *Photo Hirmer Archives Munich.*

175 Capua, near Naples. Apse fresco in S. Angelo in Formis. Christ in Glory (detail). *c.* AD 1060. *Photo Mansell/Anderson.*

176 Rome. Wall painting in the Lower Church of Saint Clemente. The Miracle of the Submarine Tomb. AD *c.* 1100. *Photo Mansell/Alinari.*

177 Ferentillo, near Terni. Wall painting in the nave of S. Pietro a Valle. Adam naming the animals. Last quarter 12th century.

178 Rocamadour. Wall painting in the Grotto of Saint-Amadour. The Annunciation and the Visitation.

179 Berzé-la-Ville. Apse wall painting in the monastic chapel. The Martyrdom of St Lawrence. Mid 12th century (?). *Photo Devinoy.*

180 Le Puy. Wall painting in north transept gallery of the Cathedral. St Michael vanquishing the Dragon. About 16 ft. high (4·88 m.)

181 Berzé-la-Ville. Wall painting in apse of the monastic chapel. Christ in Glory. Early 12th century.

182 Poitiers. Wall painting on west wall of the Baptistry. Crowned horseman. 12th century.

183 Chemille-sur-Indrois. Wall painting in Chapel of Le Liget. The Deposition. 12th century.

184 Saint-Savin-sur-Gartempe. Wall painting in nave of the church. Building of the Tower of Babel. Early 12th century.

185 Tavant. Wall painting in the Church of St Nicholas. David playing the harp. 12th century.

186 Canterbury. Wall painting in St Gabriel's Chapel, Canterbury Cathedral. Birth and Naming of John the Baptist. Mid 12th century. *Photo Courtauld Institute of Art.*

187 Hardham, Sussex. Wall painting in the chancel of St Botolph. Adam and Eve. Late 11th century. *Photo Courtauld Institute of Art.*

188 Kempley, Gloucestershire. Wall painting of Apostles. 12th century. *Photo National Monuments Record.*

189 Canterbury. Wall painting on east wall, St Anselm's Chapel, Canterbury Cathedral. St Paul and the Viper. Mid 12th century. 69 in.×66 in. (155×154 cm.) *Photo Victoria and Albert Museum, London.*

190 Winchester. The Mouth of Hell, from the Winchester Psalter. *c.* AD 1150–60. British Museum, London (MS. Cotton Nero C.iv. f.39.)

191 Italo-Byzantine (?). Virgin enthroned, from the Winchester Psalter. Third quarter of 12th century. 12¾ in.×9 in. (32·5×22·9 cm.) British Museum, London (MS. Cotton Nero C.iv. f.30.)

192 Winchester. Initial with Samson fighting a bear and lion to defend a lamb, from the Great Bible. AD 1140–60. Winchester Cathedral Library. *Photo John Webb.*

193 Catalan. Apse wall painting from San Clemente de Tahull. Christ in Glory surrounded by angels holding symbols of the Evangelists. AD 1123. Museo de Arte de Catalũne, Barcelona. *Photo Hirmer Archives Munich.*

194 Catalan. The Four Riders of the Apocalypse, from the Commentary on the Apolcalypse of Beatus of Liébana. AD 1086. Cathedral Library, Burgo de Osma. *Photo Hirmer Archives Munich.*

195 León. Wall painting in vault of the Panteón de los Reyes. Christ in Glory. AD 1157–88. *Photo Hirmer Archives Munich.*

196 Nerezi, Macedonia. Wall painting in the Church of Nerezi. The Lamentation. (detail). AD 1164. *Photo Josephine Powell.*

197 Nerezi, Macedonia. Wall painting in the Church of Nerezi. A saint. AD 1164. *Photo Department of Ancient Monuments, Macedonia.*

198 Byzantine. Icon of 'Our Lady of Vladimir'. *c.* AD 1125. 44½×26¾ in. (113×68 cm.) Tretyakov Gallery, Moscow.

199 Nerezi, Macedonia. Wall painting in the Church of Nerezi. The Deposition. AD 1164. *Photo Josephine Powell.*

200 Kurbinovo. Wall painting of the Anastasis. AD 1191. *Photo R. Hoddinott.*

201 Vladimir. Wall painting in the Cathedral of the Assumption. The last Judgement (detail of Jacob, Isaac and Abraham). *c.* AD 1193. *Photo Gasilov, Leningrad.*

202 Mileševo. Wall painting in the Monastery Church. The Resurrection. AD 1235. After Okunev.

203 Mileševo. Wall painting in the Monastery Church. The Annunciation (detail of Virgin's head). AD 1235. *Photo Collection de l'École des Hautes Études.*

204 Mileševo. Wall painting in the Monastery Church. The Deposition (detail). AD 1235. *Photo Toso Dabac.*

205 Sopoćani. Wall painting in the Monastery Church. St John (detail). *c.* AD 1265. *Photo Toso Dabac.*

206 Sopoćani. Wall painting in the Monastery Church. The Nativity. *c.* AD 1265. *Photo Arts Council of Great Britain.*

207 Sopoćani. Wall painting in the Monastery Church. Christ's appearance to the Two Maries. *c.* AD 1265. *Photo Toso Dabac.*

208 Boiana, near Sofia. Wall painting of Christ in the Temple (detail of head of Christ). AD 1259. *Photo Musée Nationale d'Archéologie, Sofia.*

209 Trebizond. Wall painting in the Church of Hagia Sophia. The Expulsion of a Devil from a Daughter of the Woman of Canaan. 13th century. *Photo Russell Trust.*

210 Trebizond. Wall painting in the Church of Hagia Sophia. The Feeding of the Five Thousand (detail of head of Christ). 13th century. *Photo the author.*

211 Trebizond. Wall painting in the Church of Hagia Sophia. The Feeding of the Five Thousand (detail of a head). 13th century. *Photo the author.*

212 Kiev. Wall painting in Cathedral of Hagia Sophia. The four daughters of Yaroslav I. *c.* AD 1045.

213 Nereditsa. Interior of the Church of the Saviour. AD 1199. *Photo Gasilov, Leningrad.*

214 Constantinople. Mosaic in the Church of Kariye Camii. The Marriage at Cana. *c.* AD 1315. *Photo Hirmer Archives Munich.*

215 Constantinople. Mosaic in the Church of Kariye Camii. Joseph's Dream and the journey to Bethlehem. *c.* AD 1315. *Photo Hirmer Archives Munich.*

216 Constantinople. Wall painting in the Church of Kariye Camii. The Anastasis (detail). *c.* AD 1320. *Photo Byzantine Institute, Washington.*

217 Constantinople. Mosaic in the Church of Kariye Camii. Theodore Metochites before Christ. *c.* AD 1310. *Photo Hirmer Archives Munich.*

218 Ochrid. Reverse of double-sided icon with the Annunciation. Early 14th century. $36\frac{1}{4} \times 26\frac{3}{4}$ in. (92×68 cm.) Skoplje Museum. *Photo Byzantine Exhibition, Edinburgh.*

219 Byzantine (?). Christ between the Virgin and St John, from the Psalter of Melissenda. British Museum, London. (MS. Egerton 1139 f.12v.)

220 Poitiers. Great East Window of the Cathedral. The Crucifixion. *Photo Archives Photographiques.*

221 Chartres. Stained glass in north transept of the Cathedral. King David. Early thirteenth century. *Photo Arthaud.*

222 Chartres. Stained glass in south transept of the Cathedral. The Nativity. 12th century. *Photo Arthaud.*

223 Canterbury. Stained glass in aisle, Trinity Chapel. Early 13th century. *Photo Martin Hürlimann.*

224 English. The Crucifixion, from the Psalter of Robert de Lindeseye. *c.* AD 1220. Society of Antiquaries, London (Folio 35v.)

225 English. Border illumination from the Tenyson Psalter. *c.* AD 1280. British Museum, London (MS. Add. 24686 f.17r.)

226 French. The Agony in the Garden, from the Ingeborg Psalter. *c.* AD 1213. Musée Condé, Chantilly. *Photo Giraudon.*

227 Cimabue. Madonna and Child with Saints (S. Trinità Madonna). *c.* AD 1285. Panel. $151\frac{5}{8} \times 87\frac{3}{4}$ in. (385×228 cm.) Uffizi, Florence.

228 Rome. Wall painting in Church of SS. Quattro Coronati. Emperor Constantine and Pope Sylvester. 13th century. *Photo Mansell/Alinari.*

229 Aquileia. Wall painting in the crypt of the Cathedral. The Deposition. Probably early 13th century. *Photo Mansell/Alinari.*

230 Parma. Wall painting in the Baptistry. Balaam. *c.* AD 1270. Photo Luigi Vaghi.

231 Berlinghieri. Crucifix. 13th century. Pinacoteca, Lucca.

232 Giunta Pisano. Crucifix. 13th century. Church of S. Matteo, Pisa. *Photo Scala.*

233 Pietro Cavallini. Mosaic in S. Maria in Trastevere, Rome. The Birth of the Virgin. *c.* AD 1291. *Photo Gabinetto Fotografico Nazionale.*

234 Pietro Cavallini. Wall painting in the Convent of S. Cecilia, Rome. The Apostles John and James, from the Last Judgement. AD 1291–3. *Photo Gabinetto Fotografico Nazionale.*

235 Detail from plate 234.

236 Cimabue. St Francis, from the Madonna of St Francis in the Lower Church of S. Francesco, Assisi. Late 13th century. *Photo Marzari.*

237 Duccio. The Madonna in Majesty. (Rucellai Madonna). Late 13th century. Panel. $177\frac{1}{8} \times 114\frac{1}{8}$ in. (450×290 cm.) Uffizi, Florence.

238 Giotto. The Madonna in Majesty. (Ognissanti Madonna). *c.* 1310. Panel. $128 \times 80\frac{1}{4}$ in. (325×204 cm.)

Index

Numbers in italics refer to illustrations